'Half My Life'

The Story of

Sabine Baring-Gould and Grace

by
Keith Lister

To Derek & Joyce

Best Wishes

Keith Lister

2002

Published by,
Charnwood Publications.
13, Grove Road,
Horbury,
Wakefield,
West Yorkshire,
WF4 6AG.
E-mail keith@listerk.freeserve.co.uk

Copies of this book may be ordered from the above address.

Front Cover: Lew Trenchard House, Devon.
By kind permission of James and Sue Murray

Typesetting by: Write Lines in Print @ Yorkshire Art Circus,
                Glasshoughton Cultural Industries, School Lane,
                Glasshoughton, Castleford WF10 4QH
                Tel: 01977-550401

Printed by: FM Repro Ltd, Repro House, 69 Lumb Lane,
                Roberttown, Liversedge WF15 7NB
                Tel: 01924-411011

ISBN 1 903833 28 0   Hardback
ISBN 1 903833 29 9   Paperback

To my dear wife

Sylvia

Contents

Foreword

Baring-Gould has been the subject of three previous biographies, published 45, 30 and 5 years ago respectively. The question has to be asked: 'Why another?'; and 'Why so soon?' The specific answer in relation to the latter is that this one was already well in hand when Harold Kirk-Smith's book was printed. Indeed the queue has not shortened: the writer of this note has heard in recent months that a major publisher is planning yet another!

All this points to a couple of undoubted facts – one, that there is a revival in the man and his multi-faceted life; the other, that just as his own two-volume autobiography left a third waiting to be published, so no biographer since has been able to unmask 'the whole man'. Certainly the prime collector of the old 'songs of the west', the writer of one of the church's best-known hymns, the last rated bearer of G M Trevelyan's descriptive soubriquet 'squarson', and the successful re-inventor of the Yorkshire mill girl to be the 'half of his life' and his 'fair lady' – Baring-Gould has remained remarkably elusive.

Keith Lister, a former policeman, has taken up the challenge of running his man to ground, and as a Yorkshireman who knows the value of 'a good woman' (as the Dedication bears witness) has sought to give Grace Taylor the place she deserves in the story. He has brought his investigative skills to bear, with thoroughness and persistence, in unearthing new evidence, clarifying some old puzzles, and presenting his materials, documentary and visual, with a fresh impact and a light touch. This work has the added bonus of being a breakaway from clerical authorship.

I therefore warmly commend this volume to family, friends, 'fans' – and critics, alike.

David Shacklock.

Preface

The name Sabine Baring-Gould is synonymous with the hymn Onward Christian Soldiers and is particularly well known in many schools and churches around Yorkshire and Devon.

Prior to commencing this biography my knowledge of Baring-Gould did not extend beyond the fact that during the 1860's he had been a curate in my home Town of Horbury and had married a local girl by the name of Grace Taylor. After consulting Crockford's Clerical Directory and Who Was Who, it was clear that the range and volume of Baring-Gould's literary work was something special. I was determined to know more.

When I met Dr Merriol Baring-Gould Almond, the present owner of the Baring-Gould Estate, Lew Trenchard, Devon, I was kindly allowed access to family papers. To achieve a balanced picture of my subject I ignored previous biographies and consulted many of the hundreds of books and articles written by him and wherever possible used his personal account of events and set them in context. I visited archives across the country, parishes where he worked and areas associated with his novels and travel guides. I also visited Europe where he travelled widely as a boy and the United States where several of his descendants now live.

I have been privileged to arrange the first meeting between descendants of both families, held in the mission that Baring-Gould was instrumental in building at Horbury Bridge in 1865. I also accompanied relatives and friends along the processional route where Onward Christian Soldiers was first sung, and to St Peter's Church, Horbury where Sabine and Grace were married in 1868.

Along with my wife I have fond memories of meeting the late Cicely (Image) Briggs who was Baring-Gould's granddaughter, and also Bertha Brown of Devon who in her hundredth year has kindly provided personal recollections of the Baring-Gould family and those of her father who was employed at Lew Trenchard.

My research has revealed previously undiscovered material about Baring-Gould's general activities, his time as a young curate, and his wide range of interests and local associates. Also of his meeting with Grace who provided him with fifteen fine children. The discovery of Grace's letters to her family provide an insight into her remarkable life in which she was virtually elevated from rags to riches and played a pivotal role in the life of her famous husband.

Keith Lister.

Illustrations

23   The Quarry Hill section of the processional route to St Peter's Church, Horbury. The sandstone quarry on the left was owned by George Frederick Knowles who donated the stone to build the Brig Mission. C.M. Cudworth Collection.

24   A typical Whitsuntide procession. The marchers are crossing New Road into Walker Lane, Horbury, circa 1908. C.M. Cudworth Collection.

25   Whitsuntide marchers at Stonecliff House, Horbury Brig, circa 1900. By kind permission of H.D. Elgood.

26   The Millennium procession approaching the south door of St Peter's Church, Horbury.

27   The Brig Mission Chapel-Schoolroom & vestry. The former Cottage Mission is rear left.

28   Sir Arthur Sullivan, circa 1870. By kind permission of Peter Joslin.

29   The first verse of Onward Christian Soldiers in Baring-Gould's handwriting. SBGAS Newsletter

30   Joseph Taylor (1823-1904), by kind pemission of Ivor Atkins.

31   Joseph Taylor lived with his family at Bank Hey Bottom, Barkisland, over-looking Ripponden and the Ryburn Valley. (Probably the cottage on the left).

32   Recently demolished cottages in the Mill Fold, Horbury Brig, where the Taylor family lived after leaving Barkisland.

33   Golden Square, Horbury, where the Taylor family lived in 1861. C.M. Cudworth collection.

34   Richard Poppleton J.P., Mill Owner & Church Warden at St Peter's Church, Horbury. C.M. Cudworth collection.

35   The Reverend James Matcham Gatrill (1834-1918).

36   Map of Dalton in 1850. By kind permission of Leeds Library, and Ordnance Survey.

37   The Church of St John the Evangelist Dalton, built in 1868.

38   Wedding register entry for the marriage of Sabine Baring-Gould and Grace Taylor at St Peter's Church, Horbury. By kind permission of the Parish Church of St Peter, Horbury, H.M.S.O. Agreement no. 20020338 & West Yorkshire Archive Service ref. WDP135.1/3/3 p. 136.

39   Grace Baring-Gould.

40   The former Whittakers Clerical Hotel, Great Russell Street, where the Baring-Goulds lodged when visiting London.

41   Le Defille des Anglais by S. Baring-Gould: Cliff Castles & Cave Dwellings of Europe.

42   Watercolour painting of Pentelstein by S. Baring-Gould. By kind permission of Ann Goldsworthy.

43   The old pulpit at Kenton Church, Devon.

44 The 'restored' pulpit at Kenton Church that was removed and replaced by the old one.
45 Thomas Waller Gissing (1829-1870).
46 George Robert Gissing (1857-1903).
47 The Wakefield Industrial and Fine Art Exhibition of 1865 was held in the building with the flag where the Town Hall now stands. The Mechanics Institute where Baring-Gould lectured is on the left. John Goodchild Collection.
48 Mersea Island, Essex, in 1884. By kind permission of Ordnance Survey.
49 The church of St Edmund King & Martyr, East Mersea, Essex.
50 The old vicarage, East Mersea, Essex. By kind permission of Mersea Island Museum Trust.
51 St Peter's Church, Lew Trenchard.
52 Memorial to Beatrice Gracieuse Baring-Gould, in St Peter's Church, Lew Trenchard.
53 The Baring-Goulds on holiday at Bude. By kind permission of Ann Goldsworthy.
54 Grace Baring-Gould with baby. By kind permission of Ann Goldsworthy.
55 Coat of arms of the Gould family.
56 Lew House after conversion.
57 The Wives of Famous Men - Mrs S. Baring-Gould (unattributed).
58 The Reverend H.F. Sheppard M.A. (1824-1901).
59 The Reverend Dr F.W. Bussell D.Mus. D.D. (1862-1944). By kind permission of the Principal and Fellows of Brasenose College.
60 John Helmore, retired miller and old Devon singer.
61 Richard Hard, retired stonebreaker and old Devon singer.
62 Contents of English Folk-Songs for Schools, by Sabine Baring-Gould and Cecil J. Sharp.
63 Hut ruin at Trewortha, Bodmin Moor, Cornwall. By kind permission of The Dartmoor Trust.
64 Baring-Gould at the entrance to Grimspound, Dartmoor in 1894, by kind permission of The Dartmoor Trust.
65 Stall Moor Circle Dartmoor, April 1894. Left to right – S Baring-Gould, J.B. Rowe, J.D. Pode and W.G. Gray (Meavy) by kind permission of The Dartmoor Trust.
66 How The Sketch newspaper portrayed Baring-Gould in 1894.
67 Shawl crocheted by Grace Taylor, for the Diamond Jubilee of Queen Victoria, by courtesy of Tulip Bemrose.
68 Three of the Baring-Gould daughters: Cicely (Mrs Tinley), Joan (Mrs Priestley) and Grace (Mrs Calmady-Hamlyn), by kind permission of Merriol Almond.

69   Baring-Gould being conveyed on his parish round by Charlie Dunstan, coach-man, by kind permission of Merriol Almond.

70   Edward Baring-Gould (1871-1957), by kind permission of Merriol Almond.

71   Dunsland House, Holsworthy, Devon, the former home of Harvey and Mary Dickinson (nee Baring-Gould), by kind permission of Merriol Almond.

72   Vera Baring-Gould (1875-1958) by kind permission of Merriol Almond.

73   Barbara Baring-Gould born in 1880 by kind permission of Ann Goldsworthy.

74   Holy Well in the garden of Lew House.

75   Squarson Baring-Gould and wife Grace, (5th & 6th from left front row), with family and staff, outside Lew House circa 1914, by kind permission of Merriol Almond.

76   The Reverend S. Baring-Gould, circa 1914 by kind permission of John Reboul.

77   The adjoining graves of Grace Baring-Gould (left) and Sabine (Right), in St Peter's Churchyard, Lew Trenchard.

78   The Memorial rood screen to Sabine Baring-Gould at St John's Church, Horbury Bridge. By kind permission of the parish of St Peter & St John, Horbury.

79   Cicely (Image) Briggs, by kind permission of her family.

80   Dr Merriol Baring-Gould Almond, the present owner of Lew Trenchard.

Acknowledgements

The writer acknowledges the kind assistance of many individuals and institutions during the writing of this book. Particular thanks are due to the following:

Dr. Merriol Almond and family for photographs and documents, the late Image Briggs, Sallie Briggs, Ann Goldsworthy, Mollie E. Priestley, Tulip Bemrose, the late Stanley Taylor, Joyce Robinson, Geoffrey Boulby, Ivor Atkins, Alice and the late Roland Hinchliffe, Mabel Stephenson, Liz Tolson, Kathleen Baldock, Colin and Freda Littlejohn, Margery Page, June Hellawell, Anne Holden, Michael Wood, Christine Cooley, May and the late Cyril Walton, John Booth, Father Aisbitt, Father Twistleton of the Parish of St Peter Horbury. Mother Robina CSPH, H.D. Elgood, Martin, Janine, and Kelly Lister, Gladys Atkinson, and the late Bella Rothery, Anne Barnes, the late Richard Woodall, Anthony Petyt, John Olsen, Susan Gamon (nee Clark), Patrick Harris, the Rev Christine Haddon-Reece, the late David Moxon, David Wilkinson, Hazel Harvey, Gilbert Venn, the Rev David Shacklock, Jim Sunnocks, Jennie Pyle, Roger & Pam Bristow, Martin Graebe, Patrick Hutton, Raymond Scott, Sybil Tope, Jane Marchand, Philip Weller, James and Sue Murray, Mrs A. Westlake, Mary Rolfe, Margaret Rowe, Bertha Brown, Martin Williams, the late Stella Stansfield, Stephanie Cassou the late John Turner, Dr's John Berry, Brian Hill and J.I. Wilson, Ossett & Horbury Methodist Circuit and Brian Smith, Eric Cudworth and Ruth Lawrence.

Joan Thornton of Yorkshire Art Circus, Ruth Harris and staff of The West Yorkshire Archive Service, Library Headquarters staff at Wakefield, Horbury & Ossett. Brotherton Library Leeds, Borthwick Institute, Record Offices in North Yorkshire, Chester, Essex and Cambridge. Royal Commission on Historical Manuscripts, the British Library, Dr Roger Schofield Clare College, Public Record Office, National Trust Killerton House, Devon. The Bodleian Library, Janet Pennington Lancing College Archive, The Mount School York, Dartmoor Preservation Association, Lambeth Palace Library, Adam Brace and John Powell of York Minster Library, Public Library & Archive New York, Houghton Library, Harvard University, the Latter-Day Saints Genealogy Society, Yorkshire Archaeological Society, John Goodchild Collection, C.M. Cudworth, Joan Wrigley, the Wakefield Express Series.

Deborah Scriven, Stella Hutchings and staff at Wakefield Local Studies Department. Also at Halifax, Huddersfield, Leeds, Bradford, Barnsley York, Plymouth, Tavistock, Torquay and Exeter.

*1. Lieutenant Edward Baring-Gould aged
30 years.*

*2. Sophia Charlotte Baring-Gould with
Sabine.*

Chapter 1

A New Direction

In May 1864 thirty-year-old Sabine Baring-Gould boarded a train north to Ripon, Yorkshire. He was a fine young man from a distinguished family and his life was about to take a new direction.

The surname Baring-Gould [1] is associated with Lew Estate, in the parish of Lew Trenchard, Devon. Once a royal manor owned by the Mules family, the property was given to the Trenchard family by Sir John Mules in the latter half of the 13th century and subsequently purchased by John Gould of Staverton, Devon in 1626.

In 1767 Margaret Gould married Charles Baring of the famous banking family and in 1795, their son William Baring, obtained a royal licence to assume the name and arms of the Gould family, thereby creating the name Baring-Gould. (See family tree appendix A).

William Baring-Gould was known as the *Devonshire Adonis* on account of his good looks and married Diana Amelia Sabine. They raised seven children and their eldest son Edward was also very handsome and nicknamed *Silver Poplar* on account of his height and fair hair. Edward joined the now defunct (1858) East India Company in 1820 and served as a lieutenant in the Madras Light Cavalry where he was described as a great horseman. Edward's career came to an abrupt end after ten years service when he dislocated his hip in a carriage accident and was discharged.

Edward returned to England and married Sophia Charlotte Bond, the daughter of Admiral Godolphin Bond R.N., at Exeter in 1832. They resided at Dix's Field in the City and on 24th January 1834 Sophia gave birth to a son who was named Sabine after his grandmother. The following year they moved to Palm Court, Bratton Clovelly, Devon, where Sophia had a second child Margaret (Sissy), followed a year later by William (Willy).

After the excitement of an active military career Edward, who politically was a Whig among Tories, soon tired of rural life. Supported by a military pension, an annuity from the sale of family property and a favourable rate of exchange, he commenced a series of four family tours around Europe which extended over a period of fifteen years.

In July 1837 Edward, his family and a servant sailed to Bordeaux and spent the next two years meandering through Baronne, Pau (winter), Bagnieres, Carcassonne and Montpelier (winter). On a second four-year tour, commencing in October 1840, the family ambled through Europe in their own coach. This time they visited Cologne (winter), Karlsruhe, Munich, Berne, Lucerne, Vevey (winter), Baveno, Milan, Salzburg, Vienna, Prague, Dresden (winter), Mannheim and Muggendorf.

When they returned to England, ten-year-old Sabine attended King's College in the Strand followed by a short period at Warwick Grammar School. On the death of Edward's father William in 1846 Edward returned to the family estate at Lew Trenchard leaving Sabine and Willy in the care of the governess Miss Richardson at Warwick. While Sabine was at Warwick he was conveyed to dancing lessons in a sedan chair and later claimed to have been one of the last persons to use that mode of transport. He was also dramatically affected by the painful death of a neighbour from cancer and couldn't understand why God suffered his creatures to endure so much pain. This event troubled him and years later he wrote *The Mystery of Suffering* [2].

In September 1847 Sabine and Willy suffered from whooping cough and joined their parents in Devon. On seeking medical advice Edward decided to take his family and friends named Snow to spend the winter in the mild climate of Pau. While they were in France the second revolution was fomenting and Edward lingered in Pau in the hope that trouble would subside. It was ironic that their rented house was close to that of the public executioner and Sabine often stared in awe at the many stone balls on the balustrade of the executioner's home, each said to represent a severed head!

By June 1848 Edward felt it was safe to return home with his family but on reaching Rochefort they were confronted by fanatics shouting death threats. Edward appealed to the English Consul for help

3. The delights of Pau, France.

and arrangements were made for their safe passage to St Malo, from where they sailed for Plymouth.

While travelling overseas, Edward had his mail forwarded from England. This included the Westminster Review and Dickens' latest novels, read eagerly in turn by all the family. Although Edward encouraged Sabine to précis his reading - something that was to be of great value to him - he was not permitted to learn things by rote and this restricted his ability to memorise poetry, lines in plays and important dates. He was also denied access to fairy tales - things that he loved.

Sabine described his father as a naturally reserved, yet formidable, character who never showed his feelings, shrank from tenderness and had no patience with weakness. He was precise and orderly and disciplined Sabine by beating him with a square ruler.

In contrast his mother Sophia, was a pretty, sweet natured woman blessed with a sensitive and caring manner. A devout and kindly woman, she spent much time in prayer and never said an unkind word of anyone. However, she was never punctual, very forgetful and untidy and Sabine inherited this latter characteristic from her.

Prior to the fourth and final European tour in October 1849, Edward let Lew House knowing they would be away for some time. At the time Sophia was pregnant again so Edward took some of the staff along to assist. These were Miss Richardson, the governess, a new tutor named Hadow and William Pengelly the groom.

This tour, like the last was also fraught with danger, but of a different kind. France was in the grip of cholera and when the family were passing through La Rochelle en route to Pau, Sabine saw a man die in the street. Spirits soon lifted however when Pengelly saw the Pyrenees for the first time and exclaimed in his broad Devon accent, *'Why, God bless my soul! Them's bigger than Dartmoor.'*

Sophia was a poor traveller and was relieved when they settled for the winter in a new, rented house on the outskirts of Pau. Her relief was short lived however,

4. Sabine Baring-Gould aged 15 years.

because Frances Trollope (1780-1863) began calling at their home. Mrs Trollope, who had been widowed, had become a popular authoress of racy books. Her presence made Sophia feel very uneasy and she related her concerns in a letter home:

I try to leave as pleasant an impression upon her mind as possible on each repeated visit that she makes, so that if she shows me up with the rest of her Pau acquaintance in her next work - and some say there is one on the stocks - she may give a pleasant portraiture of me to the world.

Fortunately Sophie's fear of being lampooned was unfounded. Frances Trollope showed a lot of interest in young Sabine, who referred to her as: *a good-humoured, clever, somewhat vulgar old lady.*

Over winter Sabine busied himself in the small English Library at Pau translating Michaud's History of the Crusades. In the spring of 1850 he discovered the remains of a Roman villa and his father helped raise public subscriptions to fund a proper excavation of the site. Alas the project foundered because of official indifference and, although Sabine was very disappointed he was delighted that his father had at last taken a personal interest in something he had done! In May that year, Sophia gave birth to her fourth and final child, Edward Drake.

The family finally returned to Devon in May 1851 at a time when agriculture was in a deep depression and the farmers and tenants were finding life particularly hard. With Lew House still occupied by a tenant, Edward rented a furnished house in nearby Tavistock.

Sabine had spent practically the whole of his youth travelling around Europe and as a consequence his education had been disjointed. Although the experience widened his horizons, gave him a working knowledge of five languages and maturity well beyond his seventeen years, there was a downside. He had

5. Clare College, Cambridge.

been denied the opportunity to make real friends of his own age, which, combined with poor health and lack of sporting activities, had restricted his social development.

At that time Sabine's interests were mainly reading the classics, history, art and religion. For one so young he had already formulated three lifetime objectives: the moral and spiritual improvement of Lew Parish, the restoration of the Parish Church and the improvement of Lew Trenchard Estate.

By 1852 Edward had taken every opportunity to suppress Sabine's leaning towards the arts in the hope that he would join the army or train as an engineer in readiness for his eventual inheritance of the three thousand acres at Lew Trenchard. The

6. King's College Chapel, Cambridge.

strategy failed and that year Sabine was admitted to Clare Hall (changed to College in 1856) Cambridge, to study the classics. Sabine's tutor was the Reverend Edward Atkinson whom he described as a quiet, good, unassuming man for whom he had the greatest respect. He also received private tuition from a Mr Rayne who, he acknowledged, did his very best to teach him Greek.

At Cambridge Sabine regularly attended prayer services at nearby King's College Chapel and was confirmed. He spent many hours reading in the college library and a friend of those days described him as: *Tall, thin, pale complexion with the sweetest face, always serene and undisturbed with an almost supernatural brightness about it.*

Sabine formed a Holy Club and when he followed his mother's example of giving to the poor, his colleagues regarded him as mad but eventually his actions became accepted and were even admired. Years later he confided to his mother that in his first year at Clare the other men had said vile and wicked things about him, making him so unhappy that he was almost in despair.

In addition to his studies, Sabine found time to write at least a dozen articles. The most popular was *The Chorister, a Tale of King's College Chapel in the Civil Wars.* This imaginative story features a chorister who saved the glass windows of the 16th century chapel from destruction by hiding them from Cromwell's forces, only to be shot before the high altar for refusing to reveal their whereabouts.

Although written as a send up, the story was popular and there were ten reprints!

While Sabine was at Clare his parents moved into Lew House and during vacations he was able to roam over nearby Dartmoor, visiting churches to sketch the ornate rood screens and pulpits. During inclement weather, Sabine delved into the complete works of Voltaire, Rousseau and Montaigne that were part of his father's comprehensive library.

Lew Estate contained a small working slate quarry and when Edward discovered that Portland cement could be produced from the dark brown slate he had a fashionable cement bath installed in the house. Sophia likened it to a grave so Edward had it decorated in bright colours and when the paint had dried the bath looked very inviting. Shortly afterwards Edward persuaded an important male guest to take a relaxing bath before dinner. Fifteen minutes later the visitor rang the bell violently to summon assistance and shouted through the keyhole to the maid *"for heaven's sake bring Mr Baring-Gould here quickly-and bring a can of turpentine."* When Edward responded, the guest cautiously opened the door and extended a strangely mottled arm to receive the turpentine.

7. Lew House circa 1805.

The paint from the bath had adhered to the whole of his body and Edward had to labour long and hard to scrub his guest clean. Shortly afterwards the bath was filled with rubble, never to see daylight again!

When Sabine was awarded his BA. degree in 1857 (MA. 1860), he said of himself: *I was bad in Latin,*

8. Sabine Baring-Gould in his late twenties.

ignorant in Greek, was no more than a child in mathematics, had a smattering of colloquial French and German, but no systematic knowledge of the literature of either nation. I was passionately fond of music, but was uninstructed in the use of pigments, and in perspective. My memory had been undeveloped. What was to become of me? Of what earthly use was I in any profession? in any course of life? I had to discover that for myself as best I might [3].

At that time Edward proposed that Sabine should join the staff at Marlborough School, where his uncle Frederick Bond was Headmaster. This did not appeal to Sabine and he offered himself for unpaid work as an assistant choirmaster at the advanced Anglo-Catholic Church of St Barnabas, Pimlico, London. The senior curate there was Charles Fuge Lowder, who had only recently returned from France after being suspended by the church following an act of urban terrorism connected with his support of Tractarian [4] principles.

Sabine lodged in Ebury Street and visited a newly built mission in the slums of the East End, where he was impressed by the good works being undertaken among the poor. He also observed the riots in 1859 that resulted in the closure of the church of St George-in-the-East.

During this period Sabine turned his back on his worried parents who only learned of his activities through his uncle Edward (General, Sir Edward Sabine K.C.B. 1788-1883, Secretary of the Royal Society) with whom he kept in touch. Eventually Sabine ran out of money and when he appealed to his father for assistance, he was refused and ordered to leave St Barnabas Church.

9. St. Barnabas Church and College, Pimlico.

Chapter 2

Teaching and Adventure

in Iceland

Determined to make his own way, Sabine was referred to the Reverend Nathaniel Woodard, a high churchman who had seen a way of linking the church with the middle classes through education. With the support of Prime Minister Gladstone, Woodard had founded his first school in 1847 and he duly appointed Sabine as a master at Lancing College.

Sabine quickly discovered that his knowledge of the classics was inadequate and within the week he transferred to Hurstpierpoint School, West Sussex that was more in keeping with his abilities. He began by teaching church principles to the 'Sons of Professional Men, Farmers and Upper Class Tradesmen' for an annual salary of twenty-five pounds. Over the next eight years he taught elementary Latin, French, German, drawing and chemistry.

Known as 'snout' on account of the shape of his aquiline nose, Sabine's eccentricities and wicked sense of humour made him a popular figure. When a bat fell down the chimney of his study he adopted it as a pet and went into class with it hanging from his gown. It came to a tragic end when the maid accidentally stepped on it!

Sabine was also renowned for taking pupils on boundless country walks across historic Wolstonbury Hill, affectionately known as Danny, which is visible from the south terrace of the school. When the 'Ruskinesque Phase' [5] was in vogue Sabine wore fashionable knee breeches, stockings, velvet coats frogged with braid and seasonally coloured ties. However, this fad ended in embarrassment when Sabine attended a dinner party wearing an inappropriate neck-tie. Perhaps this faux pas was for the best because it may have saved Sabine from being influenced by Ruskin's weird aversion to the female form!

During his time at Hurstpierpoint School Sabine planned to visit Iceland. He

10. Hurstpierpoint College West Sussex showing the dormer windows of Baring-Gould's study.

prepared himself by learning the Icelandic language and in early June 1861 engaged an Oxford man to cover his absence from school.

Sabine cut a fine figure as he stepped aboard the steam vessel Arcturus in his expeditionary outfit consisting of a jaunty Scottish cap, waterproof coat, waistcoat, knickerbockers, stockings and heavy boots. He also carried a tent, hammock, telescope, rope, opera glasses and compass kindly supplied by his Uncle Edward. Sabine had purchased his provisions from Fortnum and Mason, of London who were the acknowledged experts in such matters.

Apart from the sheer adventure of visiting Iceland, Sabine planned to collect sagas and songs based upon old-Norse mythology and had a particular interest in Grettir the Outlaw. He also took his paints along so he could develop his portfolio of watercolours.

Throughout the venture Sabine recorded his progress in letters to his family and these formed a diary of his activities. On Whit-Monday 1861 he wrote from Grangemouth;

My Dear Mama, here I am, on board the Arcturus a neat English built boat with steam screw, not much bigger than a Thames boat, no berth to be had but a sofa – 'which is unfortunate,' says the captain, 'if you are sea sick, you will spoil the gentlemen's supper,' the sofa being so close to the table.

The tiny boat was manned by seafaring Danes and the other passengers were an

American, a Frenchman, two English, a Dane who spoke Icelandic-German and two Danish women. Sabine said of one on these women; *She had a little waist round which I could put my arm twice and knot it at the side to prevent it becoming undone, she has been flirting with the cabin boy, chattering the Captain, gossiping with the dissolute Icelander and is now off helter skelter into Grangemouth to buy some bracelets or artificial flowers for her gay bonnet*

Breakfast on board the Arcturus consisted of schnapps, brandy, beer, tea, coffee, sardines, ham, tongue, black and white bread, eggs and marmalade. How much of this was actually consumed and digested is a matter for conjecture, because the passengers were constantly tossed about in the rough seas. At Thorshavn in the Faroe Islands, Sabine and the American went ashore for a meal of eggs and coffee and Sabine visited the Lutheran Church.

When they docked at Reykjavik in Iceland, Sabine hired guides and horses to carry his food and equipment and rolled his personal belongings in a bedroll, known as the black slug, which he laid across his saddle.

In those days the progress of the expedition was regulated by the amount of grass available for the horses. If the quota allocated for visitors was plentiful then they were welcome to stay. However, if it was in short supply they to had to move on. This system

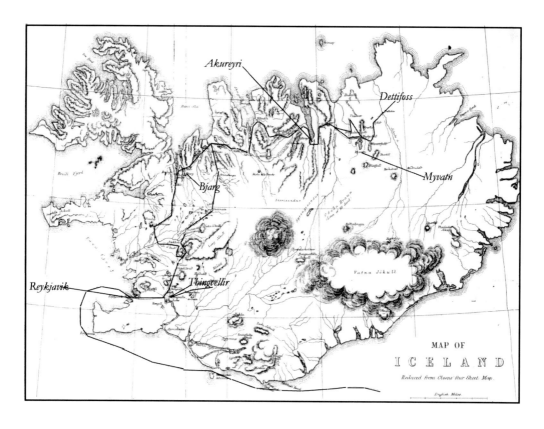

11. Map of Iceland showing SBG's route.

ensured that the lives of the local people were not put unduly at risk by a shortage of winter animal feed.

In such a wild environment the horses were a valuable commodity and while grazing they were hobbled to prevent them wandering off. Sabine quickly learned it was folly to hire a horse for less than £2 10s.0d. because it would be of little use!

During the expedition Sabine visited the site of the world's oldest parliament – the Althing at Thingvellir where the country's leaders had assembled for centuries. He found the Icelanders very friendly and joined them for religious services in the tiny protestant churches built of wooden staves. He also took a keen interest in the Danish hymns and translated one into English [6].

The Icelanders were a tall, slender people with bright complexions and a profusion of mainly brown, but occasionally red or black hair. Sabine quickly discovered that their small wooden homes were flea ridden and that skin diseases and diarrhoea were very common. He was also aware of cases of typhus, smallpox and even leprosy - imported by seafarers from foreign shores.

During the evenings Sabine was entertained by singing and recitations of the Old Norse Sagas. He showed his appreciation by handing out trinkets and after one particularly pleasant evening was about to present a cheap ring to the young daughter of his host when he was quietly warned off. On learning that such a gesture constituted an offer of marriage, and seeing that the girl was neither beautiful nor healthy, he deftly returned the ring to the depths of his bag and selected something else!

As Sabine travelled around Iceland he undertook at least fifteen watercolour paintings featuring Dettifoss Waterfall, Lake Myvatn, Oxnadalr, Vatnsdalr and Bjarg. He also painted Iceland's second city of Akureyri, which he described as: *A straggling line of tarred wooden shanties and hovels, extending along the beach, the doorsteps being just above high water mark.*

Sabine marvelled at the hot springs, saw impressive geysers, visited a grave said to contain a vampire and collected unusual varieties of wild flowers. He saw great skua and snowy owls for the first time and observed the great northern diver, gyr-falcon, ptarmigan, snipe, golden plover and huge flocks of waterfowl.

The last great auk had also been sighted there in 1844 and with a hundred pounds reward for capturing a live bird or fifty pounds for a carcass, Sabine kept a sharp lookout for one!

When the expedition ran out of meat there was none to be had anywhere. Even the birds had conveniently disappeared and the party had to be sustained by watery soup made by boiling a moss covered stone!

The remote and spectacular Dettifoss waterfall greatly impressed Sabine, whose article on it later featured in the London Illustrated News [7]. Guided by the son of one of the church archdeacons, Sabine visited the small red gabled farm at Bjarg where the Icelandic Outlaw, Grettir was born in 997 A.D. This Icelandic folk hero had been active when Christianity first reached Iceland and Sabine subsequently lectured and

12. Watercolour painting of Akureyri, Iceland by S. Baring-Gould.

wrote about Grettir's exciting and heroic adventures.

When Sabine disembarked from the Arcturus at Liverpool on 9th August 1861 he was laden with bird skins, clothes, silverware and books. He also acquired an Icelandic pony named Bottlebrush and when he rode the beast along the school drive at Hurst it suddenly stopped and stubbornly refused to move. It had never seen a tree before! Although Bottlebrush had the luxury of being put out to grass in the school field, other ponies imported at the same time were not so lucky. They were destined for the coalmines of Lancashire.

The all-inclusive cost of the expedition was £100 16s. 8d. However, Sabine also paid a further price, because on his return his eyesight had deteriorated quite badly, attributed to him reading the small print of *Rob Roy* in the boat's poorly lit cabin. Another factor may have been a deficiency of vitamin A because of a lack of fresh vegetables.

For years afterwards Sabine was never short of a good story and some were serialised in the Johnian magazine [8]. Sabine also acknowledged the support given him by his Uncle Edward and dedicated the substantial book *Iceland, its Scenes and Sagas* [9] to him. The so-called vampire's grave in Iceland also stimulated Sabine into writing *A Book of Were-Wolves* [10] and there is evidence that Bram Stoker [11] consulted Sabine's work while writing C*ount Dracula* in 1897. After much persuasion and years of translating old manuscripts, Sabine also wrote *Grettir the Outlaw* in 1890 [12].

In the decade following Sabine's visit to Iceland, it became a popular destination for those in search of adventure and diversion. William Morris, the Victorian craftsman, poet and pioneer socialist, was greatly inspired by the experience and he also returned with a collection of Norse Sagas and an Icelandic pony!

After several years at Hurst, Sabine was appointed Dormitory Master of Red Shield House and was very comfortable in his role, which brought him into contact with many leading churchmen. However, he was also constantly aware of a deep-rooted urge to be ordained. His religious development had been greatly influenced by his mother Sophia, so it was very fitting that prior to her death from cancer in 1863 she withdrew her opposition to his going into the church.

However, his father maintained that if he were ordained he would lose his inheritance and the best he could hope for, would be to follow his Uncle Charles into the living at St Peter's Church, Lew Trenchard. Apparently Sabine did not care about the inheritance but was concerned about his father's mental health and welfare and the fact that he wanted him to go to arbitration over the question of taking holy orders. In desperation Sabine sought Woodard's advice (See Appendix C) and received the terse reply: *Submit to your father.* In the turmoil of this situation Sabine came close to resigning from teaching to become a clerk of works.

Matters finally came to a head in 1864 when a vacancy arose for a chaplain at Hurst School. Although Sabine was not qualified to apply for this position he knew that his friend, the Reverend J.T. Fowler, had already been appointed to open a new church mission at Horbury Brig, Yorkshire. Working quickly, Sabine persuaded Fowler to apply for the position of chaplain at Hurst in the hope that John Sharp, the vicar of Horbury, would then accept him in Fowler's place. Sharp agreed. Fowler was duly appointed chaplain and Sabine met Bishop Robert Bickersteth of Ripon, in London and submitted himself for ordination.

A new chapter had commenced in Sabine's life and the reason for his train journey north now becomes apparent.

Chapter 3

Life in a Yorkshire Parish

Sabine wrote of his arrival in Ripon:

I took an early train and called upon the Bishop at the hour appointed, when he had just finished his breakfast; and he came in to see me, wiping some yellow egg from his lips, and a drop off his black-silk apron, on which it had been spilled. To eat an egg cleanly is a difficult operation.

He received me stiffly, being more interested in getting the drop of egg off his apron than in inquiring into my qualifications. I told him frankly that I was no Greek scholar; his mouth twitched, and a little flush came into his cheek. It was a matter of common knowledge that he knew little of it than the alphabet.

That achieved, he bade me go to Ripon for examination; he further informed me that the Ordination would take place on Whit-Sunday. The candidates would be required to lodge in the city of Ripon. His examining chaplain would furnish a list of respectable lodging-houses. Every morning they (the candidates, not the lodging-houses) would walk out to the palace, where the examination would begin at 11am.

Accordingly to Ripon I went, and at the appointed hour on the appointed day made my appearance at the Cockney-Gothic palace a mile and a half or two miles from the town. Of Bishop Bickersteth I say as little as possible.

13. Baring-Gould in 1864 aged 30 years.

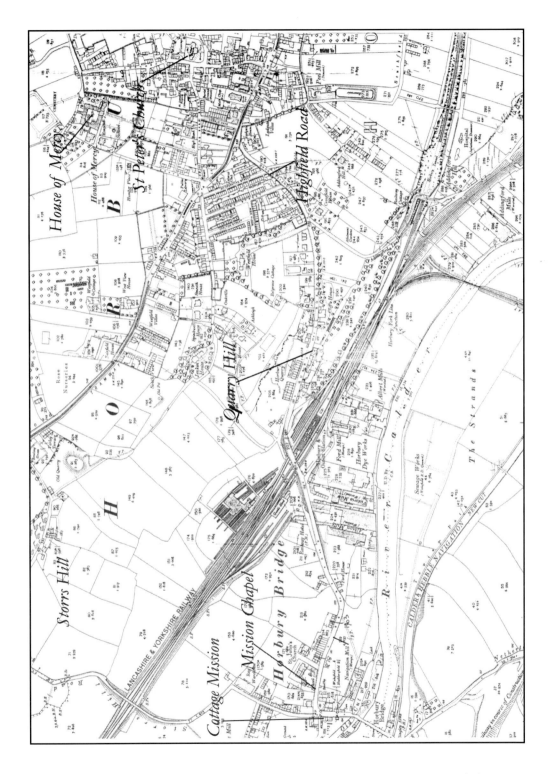

14. Map of Horbury & Horbury Bridge surveyed in 1849-51 as amended.

It is a fact that Sabine had little regard for many of the hierarchy within the church of his day – a view that he never changed.

When Sabine was ordained on Whit Sunday 15th May 1864 the process of reaching that point had caused him much heartache and personal sacrifice. However, it was a decision he was never to regret.

On Whit Monday Sabine boarded a train and travelled to his new living:

On reaching Horbury Station I found that the place provided no cabs, and possessed no omnibus. No porter was available for my portmanteau. So I shouldered it and walked up the hill towards the houses surmounted by the spire. I heard a brass band playing, and soon fell in with a procession of men. On inquiry I ascertained that this was the School Festival. So I deposited my portmanteau in a little shop, and joined the procession. What caused me some surprise was the halting, and partial dissolution of the procession at the door of the public house. But I understood that the instrumentalists, what with the ascent of the hill with the sun on their backs, and their exertion upon horns and pipes and drums, needed refreshment and called for pots of beer. I could appreciate as well the sympathy exhibited by the processionists, in that they as well called for pots of beer, to show brotherhood with the orchestra.

When, after a while, refreshed and reinvigorated, the band reformed and after a brazen flourish, blew lustily "See the Conquering Hero Comes!" I concluded that this was a delicate allusion to myself, who along with another man brought up the tail of the procession. But when the band and all who followed it passed the church and vicarage, without entering or noticing either, I began to entertain suspicions, and, turning to the man with whom I walked, I inquired as to the nature of the school in which he was, as he had confided to me, a teacher.

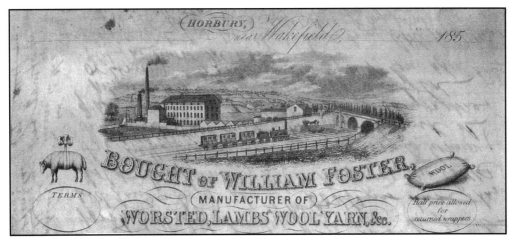

15. View of Horbury Railway Station where Baring-Gould arrived in 1864 looking from Horbury towards the Brig. In 1812 Foster's Mill had been attacked by the Luddites.

Then only did I learn that this was a Dissenting demonstration. I dropped from the tail, flew back, got my portmanteau, and stole very crestfallen into the house of the Reverend John Sharp, where I was heartily laughed at for my novel entry upon my duties.

The procession that Sabine followed was not reported in the press but the route suggests the participants were members of the Primitive Methodists, who were very active in the area at that time.

In those days the parish of Horbury included Horbury Junction and Horbury Bridge and had a combined population of around three and a half thousand. The Town was well served by roads, the Lancashire and Yorkshire Railway Company and the Calder and Hebble Navigation.

During the two and a half years that Sabine was at Horbury he lived in the vicarage in Northgate of which he wrote: *The vicarage was on the north side of the church, which cut the sun from all the windows on the South side. It possessed a small walled garden to the east, the grass, shrubs and the flowers, so begrimed with soot as to dirty the fingers that touched them. There was also an old mulberry tree in it, but the fruit tasted of smoke.*

The six-bedroom vicarage accommodated John Sharp the perpetual curate (often referred to as vicar) who was a bachelor, Alfred Davies the senior curate, William Cass the curate at St Michael's Church, Wakefield, and Sabine. There was also a schoolmaster named Charles Dutton, and a resident housekeeper. The vicar also entertained many visitors from the Oxford Movement, including his good friend J.B. Dykes [13] a well-known composer of hymns. One of his tunes entitled *Horbury* is wedded to the hymn, *Nearer My God to Thee.*

The old mulberry tree that Sabine refers to in the vicarage garden appears to have been swept away when

16. St Peter's Church and the former vicarage from the south. Ranter's Fold is to the left of the vicarage.

the new vicarage was built in 1970.

The present Georgian parish church is dedicated to St Peter and St Leonard and was built by John Carr [14] between 1791-3 to replace an earlier Norman structure. Sabine describes it:

The parish church of Horbury stands in the middle of the townlet. It was erected by a Mr Carr, an architect, at his own expense in the eighteenth century, and possesses a respectable tower and spire. Internally it has no aisles, and is apsidal [domed] at each end. This construction has its disadvantage, for every sound produced at the West end rings in the ears of the clergy within the altar rails. Thus, when a mother, sitting under the organ loft at the further extremity of the Church, admonishes her son: 'Blow your nose, and don't shuffle!' the priest at the altar receives this injunction as though personally rebuked!

The acoustic properties of the church remain much as they were in 1864 and the crypt contains the body of John Carr.

Father John Sharp M.A. (1810-1903) came from a line of distinguished churchmen

17. *Father John Sharp M.A., the Perpetual Curate of Horbury, during the years 1834-1899.*

and was appointed in 1834 by his father, Samuel Sharp M.A., Vicar of Wakefield. John Sharp was a man of action and resolve and became the foremost high churchman in the north of England.

After his appointment, John Sharp fought a long and expensive, but ultimately successful battle for the removal of the church box pews. He was also well connected with the wealthy residents of the County and with their support he opened church missions at Horbury Brig and at Horbury Junction and subsequently replaced them with parish churches. He also introduced Day and Sunday schools and four almshouses known as St Leonard's Hospital.

Most ambitious of all,

was the development of a penitentiary known as the House of Mercy. This opened in Millfield Road, Horbury Junction in 1858 and had the financial backing of Sharp's cousin, Miss Henrietta Farrer of Clapham, North Yorkshire.

The aim of this establishment was: *To rescue from sin and destruction the increasing multitude of fallen women who throng the towns and too often the larger villages of this great and populous county.* The penitentiary was so successful that a new building was commenced in Northgate in July 1862. It stood in four acres of prime land purchased for the sum of six hundred pounds from the still active Horbury Allotment Society.

Although John Sharp was appointed Warden, he delegated day-to-day management to his senior curate and a team of Anglican sisters led by Mother Superior Frances Ellen White. When the new building opened in 1864 it provided thirty beds for the female inmates, who were mainly young prostitutes rescued from the streets of London and the provincial cities. The regime quickly achieved a success rate of over 80% and the penitentiary became a model of excellence for other similar establishments.

Over several years a large complex consisting of convent, chapel, school, hospital and retreat for the clergy was developed at a cost of over thirty thousand pounds and completely dominated the northern aspect of the town.

The nature of the work undertaken there, its location and its being surrounded by

18. The House of Mercy Horbury later renamed St Peter's Convent.

a high boundary wall all combined to create an air of remoteness and foreboding. Many local women brought up in the early part of the twentieth century still recall the awful threat of being sent there if caught misbehaving!

Father John Sharp was a powerful and resourceful man and while those who opposed him often went out of business, it is known that he cared about the town and its people, treated his curates well and trusted them to get on with the job. He was a great believer in regular visits to the homes of his parishioners and this was a practice that Sabine adopted and perpetuated throughout his own long ministry.

Initially Sabine worked alongside Alfred Davies, the senior curate and sub-warden at the House of Mercy. An entry in the convent records reveal that Sharp, Davies and Baring-Gould were present in the chapel on 22nd November 1865 when Sister Louisa was admitted as a probationer. She later became mother superior there.

Sabine described his colleague Davies as: *A sound practical individual, a good theologian, who exercised much influence over the factory lasses. Not a good preacher but a wise guide of souls and as such esteemed. A believer in homoeopathy, somewhat frail of health he stooped and had a shuffling gait and hesitation in his speech. He wore a red beard and moustache and sandy hair that grew in a tangle.*

As Sabine travelled around the parish he found the broad Yorkshire dialect difficult to understand. However, he persisted and chatted to the old timers who regaled him with amusing tales and told him of local customs and superstitions. He clearly enjoyed these lively sessions and recorded them for future publication.

The first recorded funeral service that Sabine conducted was of one Nancy Turton. He wrote of the funeral tea:

A funeral feast was a great function. The table was spread with plum-cake, parkin or pepper cake, and jugs of ale. Along with the cake were served junks [chunks] *of cheese.*

Although this menu was discontinued long ago, local people still enjoy eating cheese with fruitcake, mince pies, apple and even fish and chips. Sabine also discovered that it was customary to leave the door of the house unlocked for seven nights after a funeral so that the deceased would not feel that the dear old home had been closed to them, thereby expressing the warmth and tenderness of Yorkshire hearts and their family affections.

Two weeks later Sabine baptised John Walton Adamson. Although it was not applicable in this case, Sabine knew that no parent wanted their child to be the first baptised in a new font because it was believed they would go to the devil!

It was the 9th September 1865 when Sabine gave his first sermon at the Lady Chapel, Alverthorpe, Wakefield. The theme was *On the Dedication of the Whole Heart of God* and after repeating it two days later at St Peter's Church Stanley, he was well prepared to deliver it on home ground.

Other local churches where Sabine preached were: St Andrew's at Thornes,

St Michaels, Westgate, Wakefield Prison Chapel, the Mission Chapel at Wrenthorpe, St Mary's Outwood, St Mary's at Allerton Bywater and St Barnabas' at Holbeck, Leeds.

Father John Sharp took the welfare of his parishioners to heart and provided them with clothing and savings clubs, a special sick club for women and children, a library and a parish magazine. Concerts with singing and glees were also organised in the Church Institute along with penny readings. Some of the more controversial readings attracted as many as five hundred people and it was not unknown for the parish constable to be called to restore order. This is a typical programme of events:

Penny Readings Programme [15]

Date	Reader	Subject
4 Jan	Wm Mortimer	Magnitude & Minuteness by S Larder
1866	**Reverend S.B-Gould**	The Two Miss Smiths – Unknown
	Dawson Quarmby	Tommy Toddlers Visit to the Seaside by T Toddler
9 Jan	B Cardwell	The Factory Child in homely Garb by T Taylor
1866	Reverend J Sharp	Speech of Mark Antony in Shakespeare's J Caesar
	B Cardwell	The Musical Butcher - Unknown
	Wm Lupton	The Husbandman's Arithmetic - Unknown

In September 1864 Sabine was invited to speak at St Michael's Church, Wakefield about his visit to Iceland. The subject was well received and in due course he prepared other topics including:

- *Pictures of Iceland,* prepared from his portfolio of watercolours.
- *Household Tales,* in which he disputed the stories of William Tell and Llewelln and dog Gelert, on the grounds the stories were pure myth and derived from an early Chinese book.
- The *Church Underground,* featuring monumental inscriptions and the mode of burial in the catacombs of Rome.
- The Faroe Islands.
- Unsolved Mysteries.

When Sabine attended the Wakefield Mechanics Institute in January 1867 his subject was the Faroe Isles. He explained that the tiny capital of Thorshavn could have been contained within the area of Wakefield parish church. In a vote of thanks Mr T.W. Gissing [16] paid tribute to Sabine's almost European reputation as a speaker.

On a second visit to the Institute the following year Sabine's subject was *Unsolved Mysteries* in which he disputed whether King Harold was actually killed at Hastings and if Joan of Arc was really burnt at the stake. He also raised doubts about the man in the iron mask and the fall of Napoleon! This lecture was well received and in due course the committee purchased at least twenty of Sabine's books for the members' library.

Sabine's reputation as a good speaker was growing and he received bookings from Bradford, Leeds, York, Middlesborough, West Sussex and London.

Chapter 4

The Mission

at Horbury Brig

It quickly became apparent to John Sharp that Sabine was the ideal man to open a mission at the Brig and he dispatched him there in mid 1864.

The community of Horbury Bridge (formerly and still known as the Brig) is situated in the Calder valley at a point where the Wakefield to Huddersfield road (A642) bridges the River Calder and the Calder and Hebble Navigation.

When Sabine went there the resident population was only about seven hundred but each day hundreds of workers travelled in from the surrounding areas of Shitlington[17], Ossett and Thornhill. The woollen mills were the major source of employment and as the mill girls in wooden clogs made their way to work through the village they clattered noisily along the sandstone pavements. Other employment included coal mining, stone quarrying and the transportation of raw materials and manufactured goods by road, rail and water.

For such a small place the Brig had four public houses: The Bingley Arms, The Ship Inn, The Railway Hotel and The Horse & Jockey that were all well used. For almost twenty years the church and the Temperance Society had been very concerned about the general welfare of the residents and a break-through occurred in 1864 when The Additional Curates Society [18] granted John Sharp sixty pounds per annum toward the employment of a curate.

Sabine became that curate and when he arrived at the Brig his brief was: *To work among the people who had been wholly neglected even by the dissenters and to do what he could towards the building of a school-chapel there.*

In July 1864 Sabine wrote to the Church Times [19] making an appeal:
.... It is proposed to start a mission there as a chapel can be provided – and it is a matter of urgent necessity that one should be erected this summer. The chapel

is to be built of wood, and will cost £100, plastered within, roofed with felt, and capable of containing over 100 people. Will anyone out of charity and for the love of God assist in this work? £30 has already been raised, but there is a difficulty in procuring more.

I remain yours truly,
S. Baring-Gould.
Asst curate of Horbury 27 June 1864.

On 12 July 1864 Sabine wrote to Church Times again indicating that he had received only two donations, one of a shilling and another of five shillings! He then described at some length what he was trying to do:

....We are very moderate in our demands only wanting £100 to build with, one cannot do much for that sum, but one can get under cover and that is all I ask for. If there were only a cottage which might be hired, I should be quite content with that but there is not a [vacant] cottage in the place....

This appeal also appears to have fallen on stony ground and on 30th July 1864 he wrote again:

.... it may interest your readers to know that some maidens have taken the Mission in hand, and quite of their own accord, have determined on raising a sum of money to furnish the Mission with a bell, by the sale of worsted stockings etc. which they are busily engaged in knitting. If anyone wants a dozen stockings for the winter and will send me the size of his foot, I will take his order to the bonnie lasses, and see that it is executed....

....to those who have not as yet done anything for the Mission, let me suggest that twelve postage stamps are a trifle to the giver, but that twenty such donations make a pound, which is a great deal to the receiver.

I am, Sir, yours faithfully
S. Baring-Gould.

While the appeal was ongoing Sabine appears to have held the first few meetings at the home of the village shopkeeper, Thomas Cardwell, who lived in Clock Row [20]. A boy who went there recalled perching on a three-legged table with his friends and when they were told to say 'Amen', they often shouted far more loudly than required!

The Cardwell's home soon became overcrowded and Sabine eventually rented a three-roomed cottage situated two doors away from the Horse & Jockey Public House.

During his early days at the Brig, Sabine visited Hurstpierpoint School, where he described his activities:

In a few words I may give an account of the starting of our Mission at Horbury Brig near Wakefield, and give some idea of the manner in which this work has progressed during the few months it has been carried on.

The district is poor, being inhabited solely by millhands, bargemen, and colliers; there were several large manufactories in it, but the proprietors live at a distance and care little for the spiritual welfare of the hands they employ.

The Brig is well known in the neighbourhood as a lawless and godless spot, and no kind of religious influence had been brought to bear upon it. On Sunday morning the bridge over the Calder is the rendezvous for hosts of men with their dogs who come to make up matches for dog fights and dog races, take and make bets on favourites.

The afternoon is spent in these 'sports' which come off in fields by the riverside amidst crowds of boys and girls. On Passion Sunday a novel entertainment was witnessed by a gentleman who acts as church warden to the Mission - this was a woman fight; two furious females met in a ring to have a quarrel out, and the engagement was hot and exciting, they pulled out handfuls of each others hair, and scratched each others faces with their nails - their tongues wagging pretty freely all the while. There are several public houses, and the number of drunken men reeling about the streets and roads on a Sunday is exceptionally great.

This being in this condition and the place being a scandal to the neighbourhood, it was determined to start a mission in the midst of the district as soon as possible.

The Incumbent of Horbury had endeavoured for sixteen years to produce a site for a Church, but was unable to obtain any land. He now proposed to rent a portion of a field and erect a temporary wooden chapel. In the meantime a cottage was hired within two doors of the most disorderly of the public houses, this house consisted of two rooms and a wee kitchen, the bedroom upstairs was converted into a chapel, the room downstairs and the kitchen, into a school. The chapel measures 14ft by 12ft, the schoolroom 12ft by 12ft, and the kitchen 9ft by 6ft.

On St Katherine's day, in November last, the Mission was opened by a short service commencing with the Veni Creator sung by all on their knees to a tune by Mr Boyd, an old Hurst Johnian, invoking the blessing of the Holy Ghost on the work then commenced.

Night school was carried on four days a week, and the average attendance was sixty, the number of names on the books being eighty-five: but as in some mills the work is carried on night and day, and most of the scholars being 'hands' in the mills, when it was their turn to work at night, they could not come to school.

The instruction consisted of reading and writing and a little arithmetic. The young men came on two nights, and the young women on the other two. On Friday evenings we held a savings bank and obtained about thirty-five depositors, the amount of money laid by being about £1 5s 0d in the week. On Wednesday evenings we had a creed class for instruction in the articles of faith. On Sunday afternoons there was school attended by about fifty-four children, followed by a service in the chapel, consisting of metrical litany and hymns. Evening service was at 6.30 and as always crowded, the chapel, the staircase and the room downstairs being filled.

A choir has been formed and singing is remarkably good. The way in which it was collected was curious. Boys from the first took to making noises about the house, pelting the windows with mud and discharging volleys of old boots and shoes at the heads of those who attended the services. I had then to rush out of the back door, make a circuit of the house, come in the rear of the delinquents, seize on the chief offender, drag him into the house, and turn him there and then into a chorister.

For some time these wild urchins regarded it as perfectly en regle to suck toffy, or rip and eat oranges during the choir practice or during service: and I have had to pull up in the midst of a discourse to possess myself of a large moist and sticky fragment of toffy.

By degrees the most disorderly have been reduced to order, and have been taught how to behave during service. It must be remembered that these fellows had never been inside a church before, the great majority had not even attended a dissenting chapel, as there is not one in the place.

During Lent we have been holding a service on Wednesday evenings with intercessory prayer for the conversion of sinners. The congregation kneel in silence, praying for some friend who is living in mortal sin, after which they join in a general litany of intercession.

There has been abundant token that God has heard and answered this common prayer for others. A remarkable instance of God's answer to our prayers occurred shortly after the starting of the mission. One of our night scholars, a lassie of about seventeen, was dangerously ill and the doctor had given her up, declaring that she had not many days to live. On the Sunday evening we had five minutes silent prayer for her, and from that night she took a turn for the better and is now a regular attendant at the school and services.

That souls have been drawn to the love of Jesus I know well, and trust that more and more will be brought into the net of the Church, as we endeavour by all means to put the whole Mission directly into God's hands and entrust it to Him for support, desiring that the beginning and the conduct and the ending may be His, ours the work, and His the glory.

We are crowded out of our little upper room, and to open the windows involves the chance of a dead cat or a cabbage stump being flung in and descending on the head of the minister or the worshippers. On Sunday afternoons, our good church-warden stands by the door to turn the key should a drunken man attempt to enter, we have had several come in, and have found it sufficiently difficult to turn them out.

On Good Friday, one, a quaint individual who rejoiced in the name of old Nut, who is so hard that as he says 'Naw buddy has cracked me yet,' before leaving the public house proceeded to preach a sermon, which consisted as he assured his companions of three points, and they are these - first point was the driving his head through the first window pane of the inn window, and the second point was a similar proceeding with the second pane, the third shattered the last sheet of glass, and 'my he-ad is no worr for 't,' said he; 'now I'll go tut Church and see if t'Parson preaches like me.'

So he came into my chapel where the congregation was assembling to go through the Stations of the Cross. We could not get rid of him till all those upstairs came down and secured themselves in the kitchen, when Nut finding himself alone, and wondering at his solitude came staggering downstairs to go out at the door and see what had become of all the people, we shut it upon him and turned the key. When men are not so very far gone we allow them to remain, and in one instance it has resulted in a conversion.

S.B.G. [21].

The address was well received by staff, visitors and scholars alike and the collection of £2.7s.9d. was donated to the Brig Mission. It was a fair sum in those days.

The cottage mission opened on St Katherine's day 1864 to a full house and when the congregation sang hymns their voices rippled down the staircase and echoed around the house. The theme of Sabine's opening sermon was death! On the makeshift altar

19. Bridge Road, Horbury Brig, looking toward Huddersfield. The girl in the foreground is standing outside the Cottage Mission beyond the post office. The distant building in the centre is the Bingley Arms, and the Ship Inn on the extreme left. The Horse & Jockey Public House is just off the picture to the right.

upstairs was a small wooden paschal cross that Sabine had purchased in Cambridge where it had been returned for repair by the man who carved it. By sheer coincidence it had formerly been in use at Wakefield Chantry Chapel (only four miles from Horbury) where a fanatical pro-Protestant mob had thrown it from the altar during the 1850s and damaged it!

There was much to be done at the mission and Sabine had several assistants. His right hand man was George Frederick Knowles who played the American organ at the mission and lived nearby at Jenkin House from where he controlled business interests in farming, oil, stone quarrying and the Railway Hotel!

The sisters from the House of Mercy were always on hand to assist and Sabine also mentions: *Two nice young women named Rushworth, somewhat superior to the rest, who worked in the mills.* Also, *an old muffin man convert who helped to teach the boys and often had a lit*

20. *The wooden paschal cross now in use at St Peter's Church, Lew Trenchard.*

pipe in his pocket! There was some opposition from rowdies and drunken men, but Mr Scholey, a bald headed woolcomber, would stand no nonsense [22].

The congregation had a genuine thirst for knowledge and up to a hundred people a week were instructed in the three Rs. Some evenings Sabine was so exhausted that he slept in a bed-chair at the mission and was awakened early next morning by the sound of the girls going to work in the mills. He described them as: *A pretty sight going to work on Monday mornings in their clean white pinafores and scarlet, pink, or blue kerchiefs tied under the chin.*

One Saturday morning when Sabine was on duty at the savings bank he had a stomach upset for which his colleague Davies had already given him some medication at the vicarage. When Sabine collected the mission key from Mrs Caldwell he told her of his predicament and she persuaded him to take a dose of her special powder before he left.

When Sabine returned the key Mrs Cardwell apologised profusely for having mistakenly given him a dose of powerful cow-drench! After further persuasion he

21. Cattle drench!

reluctantly accepted a dose of the proper medicine and then left for the vicarage. Knowing that he faced a busy schedule the following day, Sabine's colleagues talked him into taking a further dose of chalk mixture that had lain on the top of the vicar's cupboard for a dozen years or more!

By suppertime Sabine had developed a raging thirst and when he requested the cook to prepare him some hot-spiced beer Davies exclaimed, *'You'll be dead tomorrow and then Sharp will send me down to that confounded Brig!'* Much to everyone's surprise Sabine suffered no after effects!

On Christmas Eve 1864 Sabine was in bed at the vicarage when a single bell began to toll in the adjacent church tower. Knowing it was a parish custom to announce a death by tolling the knell, he listened carefully to the code that signalled the sex and age of the deceased. The death of an adult male was announced by three strokes of the bell, repeated three times, for an adult female it was three strokes repeated twice. A number of strokes then followed to indicate the age of the deceased. As Sabine lay in bed he counted, three, three, three followed by one hundred consecutive strokes. Thinking that a male centenarian must have died without ministration Sabine opened the bedroom window just as the Sexton was leaving the belfry and inquired,

'Who is dead?'

'T'owd un. They say' sniggered the Sexton.

'But who is dead?' asked Sabine.

'T'owd chap' came the reply.

'What old man? He must be very old indeed,' replied Sabine. *'Ay he be owd; but for sure he'll give trouble yet,'* was the reply.

Sabine climbed back into bed rather puzzled and eventually fell asleep. When he related the story to his colleagues on Christmas morning he was enlightened by the news that *t'owd chap* was the devil!

Besides officiating at rites of passage, Sabine also ministered to the relatives of those killed in fatal industrial accidents or drowned in the river Calder.

When Sabine wrote *The Pennycomequicks* in 1888-9, he described the waterways at the Brig in the following terms:

The canal and the river ran side by side, with a towpath along the former; but neither were of crystalline purity, or ordinary cleanness; for into them the mills and dye-works discharged their odorous and discoloured refuse water, dense with oil and pigment, with impurities of every description and degree of nastiness. Fish had long ago deserted these waters, and if an occasional eel was caught it was inedible, so strongly did it taste of oil and dye. The Yorkshire towns and rivers have their special 'bouquet' which does not receive favourable appreciation by a stranger!

The description was very apt but fortunately the river Calder is now far cleaner because the wool and coal industries that were once the major polluters are no longer operating.

While Sabine was at the Brig he witnessed a search for a man who had been drowned in the river. Because no one knew where the man had entered the water, a lighted candle was stuck in a raft of newly baked bread and floated down the river until it came to rest. When the searchers dragged beneath it they recovered the man's body! However fanciful this story may appear it is also logical because any flotsam and jetsam naturally accumulates where eddies occur.

Other tales that Sabine collected at the Brig relate to the alleged sighting of a monstrous supernatural dog with goggle eyes, known as padfoot, said to have haunted nearby Storrs Hill. A flarecrow [scarecrow] in the same location also put the wind up a drunken man!

Another amusing story that Sabine collected concerned a local woman who thought she was about to die and said to her husband:

'Eh! Lad! I be sorry for thee. Thou'lt be so lone wi'out me. None to cook thy dinner, none to mend thy socks, none to sew on thy buttons. It duz weigh on my sperits.'

'Don't concern thyself about that,' replied he. 'I've already spoke to Marg'et Rhodes to take thy place, and she's quite agreeable.'

'Thou hast!' exclaimed the expiring wife, starting up in bed and bringing the palm of her hand with a resounding smack on the man's bald head. 'Then, I'll tell thee what, Joe, I won't dee.'

'Very Well,' answered the man, pulling out his kerchief and wiping his pate. 'If thou'st made up thy mind not to dee, I'll speak to Marg'et and put her off!'

Chapter 5

The Whitsuntide Feast

John Sharp first introduced the Whitsuntide Procession in 1840 to mark the birthday of the mother church of St Peter's and the founding of local church schools. This innovation became a popular annual event and marchers from surrounding villages met at St Peter's School at 1.30pm every Whit Tuesday.

This procession of witness consisted of up to seven hundred robed clergy, children, teachers, family and friends, who processed around Horbury behind a wooden cross. Accompanied by a local brass band, the marchers carried richly decorated banners associated with local organisations and halted at pre-determined points to sing hymns and offer prayers for God's blessing of the parish, church life and local schools.

On the weekend before Whitsuntide 1865, it was decided that members of the newly opened Brig mission should organise their own procession to St Peter's Church and Sabine was requested to produce a suitable hymn for the occasion. He duly set the words of *Onward Christian Soldiers* to Haydn's symphony in D, number 15, and had it printed immediately so that the band and children could rehearse it over the weekend.

Whitsuntide was the time when children traditionally received new or handed down clothes. However, before going out in public the children were expected to parade themselves before their elderly relatives for inspection. Although this rigmarole was usually unpopular with the boys, any embarrassment was soon forgotten when a shiny new coin was slipped into their pocket! Most parents made personal sacrifices to provide their children with new clothes and it was woe betide any children who dirtied their outfits first time on!

When Sabine heard that one of the mission girls was not attending the feast he visited her home to inquire why. Her mother explained that her daughter was not attending because she had no new clothes. Sabine looked at the girl and said, *'What more does she want; she has a nice bonnet, and looks well in it!'* Her name was Grace Taylor.

There was excitement in the air after lunch on Whit Tuesday 1865 when over a hundred children and friends assembled outside the Cottage Mission clutching a hymn sheet and a drinking mug, [23] carried in anticipation of a potation [free tea] at Horbury

Vicarage. When all was ready the brass band struck up with the new hymn, Onward Christian Soldiers and the marchers stepped out behind a strong youth, who had been specially selected to carry the weighty processional cross at the head the parade. An onlooker observed that the combination of brightly coloured fluttering banners, the uniform of the band and the gay frocks and bonnets of the girls made an unforgettable spectacle as they marched out of the village toward Horbury. Some of the older children who took part in that first procession were Elizabeth Craven, Martha Ann Dews, Thomas Graham, Eliza Jackson, Joe Walker, Grace Taylor and Oscar Berry.

Quarry Hill climbs steeply toward Horbury and, when the marchers from the Brig began to tire, they were helped by the beat of a drum to Highfield Road, where they rested. As the larger procession from St Peter's travelled up High Street, it turned left into Highfield Road then right into Park Street and the Brig contingent then fell in behind. The combined procession then travelled along Jenkin Road, Tithe Barn Street and finally into Church Street, where they filed slowly through the south door of St Peter's Church for a special service.

Once the service was over, the children were let loose in the vicarage garden where they devoured long-buns and other refreshments. During the early evening the children changed into old clothes for field games in Low Park, while their parents and friends socialised and listened to the band. The day concluded at 9 o'clock with a short service.

22. Horbury Brig Processional Cross, against a backdrop of Yorkhire Stone.

Quarry Hill, Horbury

23. The Quarry Hill section of the processional route to St Peter's Church, Horbury. The sandstone quarry on the left belonged to George Frederick Knowles who donated the stone to build the Brig Mission.

In subsequent years the Whitsuntide procession followed roughly the same pattern until a new parish church, dedicated to St John the Evangelist was consecrated at Horbury Brig in November 1884. This event coincided with the fiftieth anniversary of the arrival of Father Sharp in Horbury and Ralph Blakelock was appointed vicar there. The following year the vicar changed the day of the Brig Feast to Whit Monday. On this occasion almost two hundred people processed around the village. Afterwards, tea was provided in the mission schoolroom and games were organised on the Brig cricket field. In subsequent years the marchers were also invited to the homes of local mill owners, Richard Poppleton and John Reid.

By 1927 the Whitsuntide procession appears to have run its course being replaced by cheap day return trips to the coast costing 7/6d by train. The writing of *Onward Christian Soldiers* was celebrated at Horbury Pageant in 1946 and, although centenary celebrations were planned in 1965, it was 1989 before the procession was re-enacted. On this occasion television personality and musician Roy Castle joined the local clergy, teachers and almost three hundred local children and teachers as they recreated the event in period dress.

A similar number of supporters also took part in an ecumenical procession to celebrate the new Millennium. This procession was accompanied by a local brass band and concluded with an inspirational sermon by Right Reverend Nigel McCulloch, Bishop of Wakefield at Horbury Parish Church. The Baring-Gould Appreciation Society (SBGAS) [24] also organised a concert featuring dialect poetry, penny readings, folk

24. A typical Whitsuntide procession. The marchers are crossing
New Road, into Walker Lane, Horbury, circa 1908.

music and a number of visits to places associated with him.

In 1865 the mission at the Brig was a thriving concern and in August Sabine attended his father's second marriage. Edward's bride was the widowed Mrs Lavinia Snow (Maitland Marshall) who, as a young woman, had accompanied the Baring-Gould family to France in 1848. Lavinia had two children from her previous marriage and was to bear two more to Edward. These were Arthur (who became Sabine's curate in 1895) and Leila. Sabine and his step-mother, Lavinia, were of an age and got on really well together.

When Sabine returned to the Brig he located a plot of land known as the Meadows, on which it was planned to build a new, combined schoolroom-chapel and a house. Sabine wrote to his father informing him that he had withdrawn his savings of £200 to purchase the 1970 square yards of land from George Coe, a local corn miller. He also made an appeal for more money stating he was at his wits' end with trying to raise funds.

Sabine wrote of those days: *I had to collect money by appeals in the Church Times and to my friends and relations. A singular subscription came to me, of half a sovereign, from a man in the mills who never went to church. Not till some time after did I learn how it came to me. He had been engaged with another in fighting their respective dogs on Sunday morning, for a prize of ten shillings, and when he got it: 'It shall go the Brig Mission,' said he, and gave it me. Of the factories at Horbury Bridge, one was in Chancery [25], another belonged to the*

25. Whitsuntide marchers at Stonecliff House, Horbury, circa 1900.

Dissenters, a third had been recently built, which the owner had strained his resources to the utmost to erect, and supply with machinery, and a fourth was burnt down [26] *whilst I was founding my mission.*

We subsequently found difficulty in obtaining money sufficient to build a school-chapel though I received generous help from some of the Horbury people. Reverend Sharp also pleaded for the Mission among his many friends and admirers. Mr Knowles was the owner of a stone quarry, and generously offered to supply, free of cost, sufficient building stone for the construction of a school-chapel. For the foundation we were obliged to employ large slabs of sandstone laid upon the gravel and sand that formed the basis of the Calder Vale, and on which several factories had been erected. It was a precarious foundation, and some of the smoke chimneys of the manufactories leaned considerably.

On 16th September 1865 G.S. Lane-Fox, Lord of the Manor, laid the corner

26. The Millennium procession approaching the southern entrance to St Peter's Church, Horbury.

stone for the new mission. It was a large event attended by a wide range of people and there were banners representing the School, the choir and the Masonic movement. With building work already well under way, the following weekend Sabine went into retreat at the House of Mercy where he met the Reverend Doctor John Bacchus Dykes. He also was a high churchman and only a few years earlier had chosen to make his first confession to Father Sharp.

The Tractarians were not always popular within the Church of England and when Dykes died in 1876, aged fifty-three, it was rumoured that his death had been expedited by Bishop Baring [no relation] of Durham (1807-1879). The Bishop, who was a low churchman, had refused overworked Dykes the services of a curate unless he desisted from Tractarian rituals - something he was not prepared to do. The full circumstances only came to notice when the Reverend J.T. Fowler, published the Life and Letters of J.B. Dykes [27] in 1898. It was Fowler who had stepped aside to enable Sabine to go to Horbury in 1864.

When Sabine published his controversial views in *Church Revival* in 1914 he condemned the Anglican hierarchy for their hostility toward The Oxford Movement. The book was pointedly dedicated to his high church friends, Fowler and Gatrill.

On 24th September 1865 Sabine was ordained priest. His sponsors were Father John Sharp, Reverend Richard Burrell of Stanley, Reverend Henry Jones of Thornes and Churchwardens Richard Poppleton and John Robinson.

When the new school-chapel opened on Boxing Day 1865, it was announced that the appeal had raised the magnificent sum of £800 and that several gifts had been received. These included candlesticks and flower vases from Sir Charles Wood, M.P. for Ripon and an embroidered altar cloth worked by Miss Duncombe, daughter of the Dean of York. A large brass altar cross set with cut glass crystals was also donated by Lord of the Manor, G.S. Lane-Fox of Bramham Park, making Sabine's simple wooden cross redundant.

At the official opening on Saturday 6th January 1866, Father Sharp announced that the chapel was opening free of debt and that the Brig would eventually have its own parish. This was greeted with loud cheers. It was a memorable day and John Sharp and Sabine had every reason to be pleased with their efforts.

27. The Mission Chapel-Schoolroom and vestry. The former Cottage Mission is rear left.

Chapter 6

Onward Christian Soldiers

The original version of Onward Christian Soldiers was published under Baring-Gould's name in The Church Times on 15th October 1864. When the children of Horbury Bridge first sang it on Whit Tuesday 16th May 1865 Sabine had set it to Haydn's Symphony in D number 15.

Onward Christian Soldiers

1   Onward Christian soldiers,
Marching as to war,
With the cross of Jesus
Going on before.
Christ the Royal Master
Leads against the foe;
Forward into battle,
See, His banners go!

     Chorus
     Onward Christian Soldiers
     Marching as to war,
     With the Cross of Jesus
     Going on before.

2   At the sign of triumph
Satan's host doth flee;
On then, Christian soldiers,
On to victory.
Hell's foundations quiver
At the shout of praise;
Brothers, lift your voices,
Loud your anthems raise.

     Chorus

3   Like a mighty army
    Moves the Church of God;
    Brothers, we are treading
    Where the Saints have trod;
    We are not divided,
    All one body we,
    One in hope in doctrine
    One in charity.

Chorus

4   What the saints established
    That I hold for true,
    What the saints believed
    That believe I too.
    Long as earth endureth,
    Men that faith will hold,
    Kingdoms, nations, empires,
    In destruction rolled.

Chorus

5   Crowns and thrones may perish,
    Kingdoms rise and wane,
    But the Church of Jesus
    Constant will remain
    Gates of hell can never
    'Gainst that Church prevail;
    We have Christ's own promise,
    And that cannot fail.

Chorus

6   Onward, then ye people,
    Join our happy throng,
    Blend with ours your voices
    In the triumph song;
    Glory, laud, and honour
    Unto Christ the King;
    This through countless ages
    Men and Angels sing.

Chorus

Sabine rarely made comment about this hymn and when a member of the *Young Man Magazine* interviewed him about writing it some thirty years after the event he explained:

The thing was written in a very simple fashion, without a thought of publication. Whit-Monday is a great day for school festivals in Yorkshire, and one Whit-Monday it was arranged that our school should join forces with that of a neighbouring village. I wanted the children to sing when marching from one village to the other, but couldn't quite think of anything quite suitable, so I sat up at night resolved to write something myself. Onward Christian Soldiers was the result. It was written in great haste, and I am afraid some of the rhymes are faulty. Certainly, nothing has surprised me more than its great popularity. I don't quite remember how the thing got printed first, but I know it very soon found its way into several collections. Yes, I have written a few other hymns since then, but only two or three have become at all well known.

The children first marched to the hymn in 1865, so Sabine's memory of having written the words spontaneously was not correct because they had been published in Church Times the previous October! Clearly, when Sabine received the late request to write a hymn he must have spent his time locating and setting his pre-written words to the tune by Haydn.

There is also an assertion [28] that the real author of the hymn was a Yorkshire dialect poet named Ben Preston (1820-1902) who lived on the outskirts of Bradford. This hearsay claim is not supported by evidence and bearing in mind that Sabine had already translated an earlier hymn from Danish and given it the appropriate credit, it is highly unlikely that he would have risked plagiarising the work of another local author, thereby exposing himself to ridicule or even prosecution!

Although *Onward Christian Soldiers* was popular within Horbury Parish, it would have probably faded into obscurity without the influence of two important events. The first occurred in 1871 when Arthur Sullivan, of the Gilbert & Sullivan Operas wrote a new tune to the hymn. He named it *St Gertrude* after Mrs Gertrude Clay Ker Seymer, with whom he had spent a weekend. Sullivan

28. Sir Arthur Sullivan, circa 1870.

introduced the new tune at a Sunday morning service in St Nicholas Church, Childe Okeford, Dorset, when he accompanied the choir on the organ.

The second event was the invention of the portable organette by Ariston in 1877 when Haydn's tune was recorded on punch card. The first voice recording by Edison also used Sabine's hymn, but this time set to Sullivan's tune performed by the Elysian Singers.

The organette was soon exported around the world and Onward Christian Soldiers went with it. The hymn became popular in churches almost everywhere, with missionaries in Africa, at religious services aboard ships and by pioneers as they headed west across America by wagon train.

Although always modest about the success of Onward Christian Soldiers Sabine did occasionally boast of being able to earn a pound before breakfast by writing out a copy of the first verse for American dealers!

Although the hymn became a firm favourite, it also attracted its share of criticism. Some regarded it as shallow and smacking of popery and the pacifists disliked its war-like similes. Some hymnals omitted the fourth verse and objections were made to the line *We are not divided all one body we* - on the grounds that the Church is not one body. When Bishop Bickersteth of Exeter proposed that *With the cross of Jesus going on before* should be amended to *With our Lord and master going on before,* Sabine strongly objected. However, Sabine did permit variations in Hymns Ancient and Modern and the Fellowship Hymnbook.

Unlike the pacifists, the church militants relished the hymn's war-like similes. In 1918 a corporal in the United States Cavalry suggested in the *Trench Camp Magazine* that it should be adopted as America's Battle Hymn and wrote:

Does it not appeal to you as the battle hymn of the hour - the very thing we need - that extra something not expressed by bayonets or bursting shells, but the human dynamic force back of them [sic] inspired to an overwhelming victorious strength? Let us sing it everywhere, on the march, in the divine service, in our hearts. Let it grow and kindle within us. Let us thoroughly understand our objective in that song, so that no matter what

29. *The first verse of Onward Christian Soldiers in Baring-Gould's handwriting.*

the experience or sacrifice may be we will stick to our task with that tenacity which has ever marked American victory. Therefore, let the bands sound off - The Battle Hymn of America. Onward Christian Soldiers.

The editor of the magazine added:

His suggestion is an excellent one. No hymn is more universally sung. No hymn rings with the martial spirit as does Onward Christian Soldiers! There is dignity, a sweep of majesty in the setting that enraptures and ennobles any soul the least bit responsive to emotion. We have heard it sung by 20,000 people and the effect was tremendous. It has been sung in our hearing by small gatherings, and never does it fail to impart virility and a challenge to the holiest impulses. We heartily endorse the suggestion [29].

The same year Sabine also received a request to publish a five-stanza version of the hymn entitled Onward U.S. Soldiers. He wrote on the request:

A young lady of Kansas City sent me this asking my permission to publish it. I replied that I objected to Onward Christian Soldiers being turned into a coarse song! Sabine blocked every proposal to use the hymn in a military context.

However it was a favourite of Winston Churchill, and was played at a service of commemoration aboard the new battleship, H.M.S. Prince of Wales when he and President Roosevelt signed the Atlantic Charter in the mid-Atlantic on 15th August 1941.

In 1996 there was further controversy when Hymns Old & New introduced an alternative version written by Michael Forster entitled *Onward Christian Pilgrims*. The *Yorkshire Post* [30] *Newspaper* correspondent Malcolm Barker wrote: *Unlike the heroes of the original, the pilgrims neither march as to war nor cause hell's foundations to quiver...and limp stuff it seems compared with Baring-Gould's verses, which rollick cheerily along.* Whatever one's views, the hymn has certainly withstood the test of time!

Other hymns written by Sabine during the 1860s are: *Now the Day is Over* [31], *Through the Night of Doubt and Sorrow* [32], *On the Resurrection Morning* [33] and *Sleep my Saviour Sleep* [34]. Others not so well known [35] were, *Hail the Sign, the Sign of Jesus, There is one True, one only God, Daily, daily sing the Praises* and *My Lord in Glory Reigning*. Sabine also collected a beautiful Basque hymn entitled *Hasten to Bethlehem* [36] that was published in the newspapers shortly before his death.

The Dean and Chapter of Exeter Cathedral received autographed copies of Sabine's hymns but these were destroyed during a bombing raid in 1942.

Chapter 7

Love is in the Air

'I want someone who will save me £100 a year, not one who will spend it!'

During the 1840s Joseph Taylor (see Taylor family tree Appendix B) and his wife Hannah lived in a weaver's cottage at Bank Hey Bottom, Barkisland, Yorkshire. Their home overlooked Ripponden in the Ryburn Valley where Joseph worked as a wool comber in a textile mill. Their first child, John, was born in 1848 and Grace Berry followed on 27th March 1850. She was baptised at Ripponden Parish Church. The couple had two further children while living at Barkisland, Susan in 1852 and William in 1854.

In 1855-6 Joseph Taylor left Barkisland and followed in the footsteps of relatives named Berry [Grace's second name] by moving to Horbury, some 20 miles down the Calder Valley where the textile industry was booming. Joseph found employment at Richard Poppleton's newly opened Mill at Horbury Bridge and rented a cottage in the Mill Fold (yard) nearby.

Unfortunately there are no official records confirming Grace's childhood but her early development can be compared with that of her friend Elizabeth Wilby who lived next door in the Mill Fold. Elizabeth attended a nearby Dame School [37] run by a Miss Crowther, where, in addition to basic instruction in the three Rs, she was taught to knit and sew. At the age of five Elizabeth knitted herself two pairs of

*30. Joseph Taylor
1823-1904.*

31. Joseph Taylor lived with his family at Bank Hey Bottom, Barkisland, overlooking Ripponden and the Ryburn Valley. (Probably the cottage on the Left).

32. Recently demolished cottages in the Mill Fold, Horbury Brig, where the Taylor family lived after leaving Barkisland.

socks and, when only seven, made three shirts for her brother.

Elizabeth began work in Poppleton's worsted warehouse when she was seven, working from 6 a.m. to 6.p.m. for 2s. 6d. per week. Often she worked three evenings a week until 8.30pm, for 4d. per week extra. When the Factory Act came into force she was compelled to leave, but when ten years of age became a half-timer at nearby Baines' Mill where she met her future husband and had a family. This lifestyle, invariably linked to attendance at a local chapel or church, was typical of that of thousands of young women raised in the industrial West Riding in those days.

Shortly after the Taylors arrival at Horbury Brig, Hannah gave birth to her fifth child, Thomas, followed by Ann (1859) and Benjamin (1860). The Census records that by 1861 the Taylors had removed to a larger house in Golden Square, Horbury close to St Peter's Church, where they worshipped. In 1862 Hannah gave birth to another daughter, Mary, followed by Sarah in 1865.

Joseph was employed as a mill scourer with maximum earnings of 22 shillings for a 60-hour week. His thirteen-year old son John was a mill hand who earned approximately 10 shillings a week. Although Grace was recorded as a scholar she is known to have helped to make ends meet by tying up bundles of rags during the evenings for 4 shillings a week.

When Sabine arrived in Horbury at Whitsuntide 1864, Grace was fourteen-years old and worked at Poppleton's Mill. The mill women were generally a lively bunch and enjoyed a bit of fun. They also maintained their own pecking order and, as a junior, Grace would have been kept in check. According to local man Joe Walker, the Taylor girls were all uncommonly good looking and Grace was charming, unaffected and somewhat different from her contemporaries. He also knew that when Sabine once visited Hannah Taylor in her home because of sickness, he was very pleased to see teenage Grace baking the bread for her family [38].

According to Elizabeth Wilby, Grace became acquainted with Sabine while she was a Sunday school teacher at the Brig Mission and this coincides with Father Sharp's request for volunteers to assist Sabine at the Mission. With Grace then living close to Sabine in Golden Square they would undoubtedly have walked together along the remote Jenkin footpath to and from the Mission in the area where Padfoot is rumoured to have roamed.

Their association naturally led to gossip and the indomitable Joe Walker observed that the young vicar and the factory lass were often seen together and what fond lovers they seemed to be! Grace's elders warned her to watch her step with Sabine, because there was no shortage of examples of naive working girls who had fallen into temptation with so called gentlemen, only to be left in the lurch when they became pregnant. Those fortunate enough to be sent away to have their child usually avoided bringing shame on their families, but many were thrown out with no means of support and ended up in the gutter.

In some circles it was fashionable for gentlemen to marry working class girls. An example was the barrister and poet, A.J. Munby [39] who secretly married his maidservant,

Hannah. However, Munby was in for a shock because Hannah was a strong character who refused to become a lady! This forced him to live a complicated double life, hoping that his unsuspecting family and influential colleagues in the city would never learn of his secret life among fish girls and female acrobats! Munby's embarrassment was so acute, he left instructions in his will that his story must not be told until forty years after his death. There was no such humbug with Sabine, who behaved honourably toward Grace throughout their liaison.

Toward the end of 1865 Sabine's father summoned his sons to meet him in Devon to discuss matters concerning the estate. While they were there Willy became violent and attacked Sabine so the meeting had to be abandoned. Willy received medical attention and was sent away for five years.

When Sabine returned to Horbury he resumed his relationship with Grace and wrote a series of letters to his father. Unfortunately only one letter appears to have survived and bears the endorsement *to be kept* suggesting that the others were destroyed.

33. Golden Square, Horbury, where the Taylor Family lived in 1861.

The letter reads:

30ᵗʰ July 1866 .

My dear Father,

You need not be alarmed at my marrying without seeing my way. I only put a supposititious case, and I am not likely to take myself a wife yet a while….

I have a great hankering after B. Columbia, but I shall take a little longer to think about it. I could not go as curate to Lew - I know well that in money matters it would be better, but you know that Aunt Marianne always falls foul of the curate, and would be sure to get across with me….

The bracelet has arrived and with it what I did not want a chain and card case, however I can stow them away. Aunt Fanny has the brooch. I gave it to her but she wished it to go with the bracelet….

34. *Richard Poppleton J.P., mill owner & Church Warden at St Peter's Church, Horbury.*

Although Sabine was playing down the possibility of marriage, his diary reads: *I proposed to dear Grace and was accepted. She had nothing but she would make a good wife in the New World.*

The reference to the jewellery probably relates to the chain and neck brooch worn by Grace in the photograph on page 67. Playing down of the prospect of marriage and making applications to move overseas to British Columbia or Honolulu suggest that Sabine's normally calm and logical mind was in turmoil. He was in love!

When Sabine asked Joseph Taylor for permission to marry Grace, her mother Hannah exclaimed, *'you would surely never think of such a thing since there are plenty of girls with wealthy parents in the parish.'* *'Well,'* said Sabine, *'I want someone who will save me £100 a year, not one who will spend it!'* [40].

The couple became engaged and arrangements were made for Grace to undertake training to prepare her for the duities of a clergyman's wife.

In an undated letter, Mrs Nora Sissons, (daughter of Grace's sister Emma), wrote: *there was a lot of ill feeling among the upper classes in Horbury against the Taylor family because Sabine did not choose to marry one of their daughters. He took her away and placed her among his friends before he got married so you can understand the catish remarks,[when] he sent her away to be educated in the way of the upper classes...*

The well-informed Joe Walker said that Grace underwent two years of training in York, supplemented by a period with friends of John Sharp. Again there is no record of this, although another source suggests that Grace lived with a good local family named Charlesworth and there were several local families by that name. What is certain is that in May and June 1866 Grace attended Horbury Church and was also confirmed by the Bishop of Ripon.

For Grace to be uprooted from her family and friends and placed among strangers of another class must have been quite daunting for her. However, she was young and put her faith in Sabine who, after all, was an experienced mentor. During Grace's absence Sabine compensated Joseph for the loss of his daughter's earnings.

In those days Disraeli spoke of Two Nations: the well-to-do and those who served them. Sabine was clearly from 'Upstairs' while Grace was from 'Downstairs' and Sabine undoubtedly encountered some degree of social and professional difficulty arising from his choice of bride.

With the Brig Mission now well established the time was right for Sabine to move on and toward the end of 1866 he accepted the perpetual curacy at Dalton, North Yorkshire. It was within the gift of Lady Downe of Topcliffe who was a friend of John Sharp and a benefactor of the House of Mercy. Her Ladyship also happened to be the daughter of a bishop and had fixed views on how church matters should be organised.

The last official function attended by Sabine was at the Brig Mission on Boxing Day morning 1866. It was also the first anniversary of the opening of the mission and the Wakefield Express Newspaper [41] wrote an account of proceedings:

Reverend S. Baring-Gould who is shortly about to leave Horbury said how it was that they had got the money to build the place was more than he could tell. The school a year last Whitsuntide but one, numbered about seventy scholars, and last year the number had increased to 120 and since then it had grown to about 150. When he went down to the place at first he was told it was no use trying. There had been several previous attempts; the Primitive Methodists tried; and others had tried, but all had failed. He had, however, great confidence in the grain of mustard seed, which was Christ's Church; and God had prospered and blessed the work. Hitherto no day school had been formed, but a great desire had been expressed for this want, and one would be opened in a week or two. But even this was not all, and he hoped before long a church and parsonage house would be built, and then the Bridge would be made into a separate parish of itself. He then apologised for the absence of Reverend Gatrill, of St Barnabas's, Holbeck who was about to take his place. He also alluded to the formation of a new day school after which Reverend J. Sharp made a very humorous speech and the proceedings were brought to a close about ten o'clock.

James Matcham Gatrill, the new curate, was a thirty year-old native of Dorset and a high churchman. According to Sabine he was a quiet, studious fellow who wore a large black beard. Gatrill had previously served in Yorkshire livings at Whitechapel, Cleckheaton, and St Barnabas, Holbeck near Leeds. He became one of Sabine's closest and most trusted friends.

Grace spent the Christmas of 1866 at home with family and friends. Early in 1867 her father Joseph moved to a cottage at Spring End, Horbury which is close to the boundary with Ossett. On 21st October 1867 Hannah suddenly collapsed and died at home. She was forty-five-years old and had been married to Joseph for twenty-one years. An inquest at the King's Arms Hotel determined that her death was from natural causes and the funeral was held in nearby Northgate Cemetery. The service was conducted by Reverend Alfred Davies but it is not known whether Grace or Sabine were present. Only nine weeks later tragedy struck again when Grace's seven-year brother Benjamin also died. He was buried with his mother.

35. Reverend James Matcham Gatrill (1834-1918).

Chapter 8

Dalton & Marriage

The Post Office Directory of 1872 describes Dalton as:

a straggling village in the Thirsk Union and County Court District, situated on a branch of the Cod Beck, 1 mile west from the railway station at Sessay. There is a church lately built by Viscount Downe, not yet consecrated. There are chapels for Wesleyans and Primitive Methodists. Lord Leconfield, who is lord of the manor, and Viscount Downe, are the principal landowners. The area of the township is 1200 acres and the population in 1871 was 271.

When Sabine arrived at Dalton on Christmas Sunday 1867, he was allocated a three bed-roomed house adjacent to the site of the present church. With a stipend of £150 a year, matched by a similar amount from his father, he was financially comfortable and well able to employ a resident housekeeper.

Sabine also inherited a character called Mills, alias Brother Augustine, an unpaid servant-sacristan, who had been taken in by his predecessor. Apparently Mills had returned to this country from Rome after absconding while training to become a monk. Mills was a simple soul and Sabine took pity on him and in return for his services provided him with free board and lodgings and an occasional shilling to enable him to visit York on his day off.

While Brother Augustine was on official duties, he wore a sombre black cassock and biretta hat. On his days off, however, he caused great amusement as he walked through Dalton wearing a black frock coat, white waistcoat, straw-coloured kid gloves, silk hat that shone as if it had been oiled, with a stephanotis in his buttonhole and carrying a Malacca cane.

When Sabine arrived at Dalton religious services were held in a remote [site not known] barn-cum-chapel across the fields, of which Sabine wrote: *The rage of the winds down Swaledale in the autumn and winter was indescribable, and often I had to get to the little temporary chapel, clinging to the railings of the adjoining*

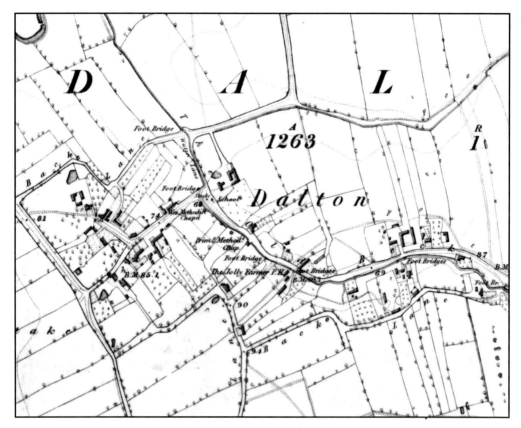

36. Map of Dalton 1850.

field, and struggling on yard after yard against the blasts of the icy gale. In such a small place, and with so few parishioners, I had plenty of time for thought and study....

The rustic congregation was so steeped in advanced ritualism that Sabine introduced some changes. One of them involved special preachers taking the mid-week services during lent. All went well until the arrival of the Reverend Richard Collins, alias Dirty Dick of Leeds who had not prepared a sermon. Sabine was greatly embarrassed when Collins began fumbling in the bible for a text and after reading out *the wages of sin is death* he waffled his way through a twenty-minute address. When members of the congregation later remarked that Muster Collins had preached a grand sermon Sabine was not amused.

The first meeting that Sabine had with clergy colleagues was his last. He was not impressed. Nor did he hold a high opinion of Archbishop Thompson of York who, he claimed, had filled all his benefices with low churchmen, because he could trust them. Sabine had little regard for most of the bishops and made the following reference to them in his Reminiscences:

There are bishops and bishops. The old bishop who was elevated from a headmastership of a public school, possessed some experience as a ruler. He had little or no spiritual experiences, but he possessed dignity and showed that he knew what he was worth. The low church bishops, none of whom had been schoolmasters, and were not even scholars, thought themselves infinitely more capable than they were. A good many bishops whose parentage was of the middle class at once developed 'swollen heads,' and exercised their authority arbitrarily and tactlessly. They were, and conducted themselves, like Mr Dorrit when he emerged from the Marshalsea and came into his property. They were Dorrit in their strut, their posturing, their self-importance, and cultivation of parasites. Strong words indeed!

While Grace was undergoing her training, Sabine had plenty of time to reflect upon what had occurred in recent months and commenced writing his first novel entitled *Through Flood and Flame*. This autobiographical and anonymous account of Sabine's time at Horbury appears to have been a cathartic exercise for him in which he expresses his feelings of tenderness toward Grace and vents his spleen on those who had irritated him.

The plot thinly disguises Horbury as Sowden and local people were given pseudonyms: Annis Greenwell [Grace Taylor], Mr Furness the vicar [Reverend John Sharp], Mr Arkwright [Richard Poppleton] and Hugh Arkwright [Sabine].

The following extract illustrates Sabine's intense feelings for Grace and makes reference to her social background:

Hugh [Sabine] *remained awake the greater part of the night immersed in anxious thought. He felt that his peace of mind was bound up with that little girl. How this had come about was more than he could tell. What it was which had influenced him he could not discover. He had been in much society, he had mingled with a great number of the other sex - yet never felt drawn to any of them in the way he was conscious of being attracted towards Annis* [Grace]. *And now his heart was full of strange cravings, his soul yearning with indescribable earnestness for one whom he had seen very little of, knew less of, who was not his equal in station and education? How was this?*

All day his thoughts were full of her, he could not sleep for trouble connected with her; her happiness was to him the dearest object of life. One glimpse of her was like a sunbeam entering a gloomy apartment and lighting it up.

The sound of her foot made his pulse leap, the touch of her hand kindled a fire in his bosom, the tone of her voice was music to his soul. I love her, I love her, and a bad job it is too.

What was Annis? A poor girl, working in a factory, without social position and education and money.

In Victorian times these passionate expressions would have been considered quite racy. They raise the question of what Grace's reaction was to her fiancé's outpourings!

In the next extract from the book Sabine describes a subtle attempt to drive a wedge between Annis [Grace] and Hugh [Sabine] when Mr Arkwright [Richard

Poppleton] asks:

'Do you not find Annis, that your way of talking is very different from ours? and do you think that you could learn to give up the old brogue for proper grammatical English? Would not you fear whenever you opened your mouth that you were saying something wrong which would make others stare and laugh, and fill you and Hugh with shame?' Annis replied, 'I do. Oh! I do indeed wi my whole heart.'

In a further example Mr Furness [John Sharp] introduces Annis to his sister and requests her to befriend and train her:

Dear Bessie,

I send you a nice little girl, an orphan, to take care of, instruct, clothe, feed, and bring up in her duty to God and man. In return, she will wait on mother and you, and make herself generally useful.

A young gentleman here, of education and good character, has lost his head to her, and I think the poor little body has lost head and heart to him in return. Of course I must do what I can to stop this, or rather direct it. Bessie, you see to her. If they forget one another, well and good. If God has joined them in heaven, man must not put them asunder, and your kind offices to the girl will have smoothed the way to the final pleasant settlement.

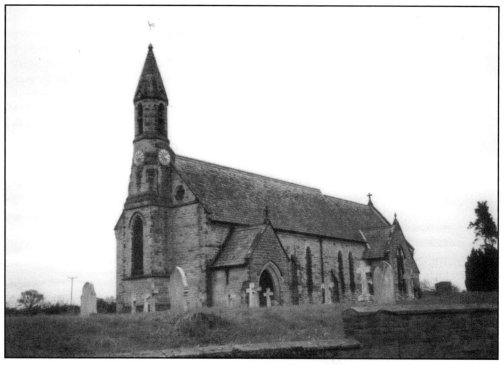

37. The Church of St John the Evangelist Dalton, built in 1868.

Certain topographical aspects of this novel are clearly constructed around factual newspaper reports of the great flood in November 1866 when the River Calder burst its banks and members of the clergy rescued victims in a boat propelled by a clothes prop. Sabine embellished events by describing the raging waters of the Calder sweeping away the Horse and Jockey Public House along with the licensee - divine retribution perhaps for those who countenanced interruptions to religious services at the Brig Mission!

Sabine also ridiculed the dissenters from Ranter's Fold, whose aptly named headquarters were within earshot of his room at the vicarage. On a point of local historical interest, Sabine also makes reference to the Halifax Building Society that had recently opened.

On his daily parish round at Dalton, Sabine visited New Mills where he saw a large barrow of earth known as Giant's Grave. He discovered that a one eyed giant had once captured a youth named Jack and made him work in the mill. When Topcliffe Fair arrived Jack wanted his freedom and waited until the giant fell asleep, then plunged the giant's sword into his eye and escaped. Sabine recognised the story as being identical to a much earlier version involving Ulysses and Polyphemus.

The battle of Brunanburgh (Boroughbridge), also occurred close to Dalton and Sabine investigated. With new evidence gathered from the Norse Sagas, he highlighted several inaccuracies in the accepted historical account [42] of events and confirmed the date of the battle as 937 A.D., a decade later than recorded. Sabine does not make any reference to the prominent White Horse of Kilburn that had only been excavated in 1857 and was probably of little historical interest to him.

During Sabine's period of incumbency at Dalton (1867-1871) Lady Downe commissioned William Butterfield to build the present church. Completed in 1868, it was built in the Early English style and was dedicated to St John the Evangelist. It has beautiful stained glass windows [43] designed by pre-Raphaelite artists William Morris, E Burne-Jones and F M Brown. Oddly, the building was never consecrated while Sabine was at Dalton and he gives no explanation for this or even mentions the church! The issue is further complicated, even today, by the total absence of any official records for that period.

On Wednesday 6th May 1868 Sabine visited Horbury to organise his marriage at St Peter's Church. It was arranged for Sunday 24th of May 1868 with readings of the Banns arranged for the 10th and 17th May and the morning of the wedding.

Normally, a man of Sabine's standing would have organised a society wedding but he must have considered this inappropriate, adding weight to the rumour that no relatives from either side were present at the wedding, because it was ill matched. In the absence of Father Sharp, who was on long-term convalescence leave in Mentone, Italy, the wedding ceremony was conducted by Sabine's colleague, Alfred Davies. It was a big occasion for Grace, who was clearly very nervous and mistakenly signed the register in her married name, necessitating an amended entry. The only known relative

No.	When Married.	Name and Surname.	Age.	Condition.	Rank or Profession.	Residence at the Time of Marriage.	Father's Name and Surname.	Rank or Profession of Father.
	1868. Marriage solemnized at *St Peter's Church* in the *Parish* of *Horbury* in the *Count.* of *York*							
316	May 24	Sabine Baring-Gould	24	Bachelor	Clerk	Dalton	Edward Baring-Gould	Gentleman
		Grace Taylor	18	Spinster		Horbury	Joseph Taylor	Dyer

Married in the *Church of Horbury* according to the Rites and Ceremonies of the *Established Church after Banns* by me. *Alfred Davies* Rd Tenate

This Marriage was solemnized between us, *Sabine Baring-Gould* / *Grace Taylor* in the Presence of us, *Catharina Winter* / *Susan Taylor*

38 Wedding register entry for the marriage of Sabine Baring-Gould and Grace Taylor at St Peter's Church, Horbury.

present was Grace's younger sister Susan, who was a witness. The second witness was a female friend out of the congregation.

Only basic details of the marriage were published in the press and the date was incorrectly quoted as the 25th May. Sabine had a problem with dates and was probably responsible for the error. He even compounded it by quoting it again in his Reminiscences! Although the entry in the Parish Magazine was accurate, it is noteworthy that there was no further greetings or general report of the event.

The couple had a month's honeymoon in fashionable Interlaken where Sabine showed Grace the beautiful scenery around the Jungfrau, Lucerne, Meiringen and Valais. They visited Rheims where Sabine bought his new bride an oil painting of the crucifixion of Christ by Lavidiere that now hangs in Lew Trenchard Church. The newly weds also visited the

39. Grace Baring-Gould.

Alpine Abbey of St Maurice where Sabine admired the portrait of St Sigismund by Paul Deschwanden, from whom he subsequently purchased another three paintings.

On the journey home there was drama in the railway carriage at Ostend when a madman cut a piece of block sugar with a bloodstained knife and offered some to Grace. When she declined it the man took offence and his eyes flared. At this point Sabine intervened in French and explained that his wife was thinking of her children. The man then placed the sugar on Grace's knees and began counting out on his fingers how many children she had. Sabine interjected again and said: *I am only newly wed and have no children but I have good insight.* At that moment, and much to his relief, a couple of gendarmes appeared and arrested the man.

The couple spent the last few days of their honeymoon at Whittaker's Clerical Hotel, Great Russell Street, a place where Sabine lodged when visiting London.

Thinking that Grace would benefit from amusement combined with instruction, Sabine took her to the Pantechnicon in Motcomb Street, where visitors were invited, *to enjoy a fascinatingly surrealist association of improbable objects.*

At this exhibition they experienced electric shocks, paraded in front of distorted mirrors and attended technical lectures. However, after an awful lunch of sandwiches as dry as boards, leathery old fowl and vinegary wine, Grace was fed-up and requested that Sabine take her to a place where amusement was not coupled with instruction.

40. *The former Whittakers Clerical Hotel, Great Russell Street, where the Baring-Goulds lodged when visiting London.*

That evening they went to the Princess Theatre to see King Lear and Grace enjoyed it. On the train home Grace said to Sabine: *I do most sincerely hope that at Dalton I may be fed with only egg-spoonfuls of instruction, and be given amusement in soup ladles!*

My Dear, you shall be fed as your constitution requires. (Alas! There was not much amusement to be obtained at Dalton-i'-t'-Muck).

You must be satisfied with what you can get, and profit by even that which is driest.

Like the sandwiches at the Pantechnicon? Grace replied.

Prior to his marriage Sabine had discharged the housekeeper and Brother Augustine, so when they arrived at Dalton, Grace was responsible for the household duties. During the early days of their marriage Sabine read to Grace as she prepared the meals in the kitchen and he studied in the evenings while Grace sat by the fireside knitting. They also kept a Persian cat that spent many hours stretched out across the warm hearthrug. When Sabine bought some geese for the garden they were attacked by foxes so he had to summon the Master of the Hounds.

Darwin's work on the *Origin of the Species* had created much interest and while Sabine was at Dalton he began writing his own version entitled *The Origin and Development of Religious Belief.* He was deeply engrossed in this work when Grace asked him to order some meat from the butcher while on a visit to Thirsk. Sabine duly complied but got the order wrong and Grace was shocked when 40 pounds of beef arrived! Over the next few weeks Sabine and Grace and their newly appointed servant girl had beef served up in every conceivable way until they loathed the sight of it. In despair, Sabine finally arranged for the choristers to polish it off at a picnic in the Hambledon Hills!

One day Sabine received a report from Doctor Mitchell that he was very perturbed by an incident that had just occurred on a home visit to a very ill and wretched old woman. The doctor explained that he had only been in the woman's house a few minutes when his dog, which had been sitting quietly outside beneath his cart occupied by his brother and sister-in-law, suddenly backed away, fur bristling as if it had seen something that had scared it out of its wits. It began howling and ran under a hedge, where it crouched with staring eyes. It then ran twice around the house at a furious pace and disappeared from sight just as the doctor left the house saying that it was all over with the old woman.

On learning what had occurred and hearing the dog howling in the distance, Doctor Mitchell had run home to collect his gun. When he discovered it crouched in a hedge, foaming at the mouth with distended eyes, fur erect and reeking with sweat, he killed it and swore his relatives to secrecy. After hearing the story Sabine determined that both dogs and horses possess the faculty to see things that are hidden from our eyes.

During Sabine's early days at Dalton the beautiful Dowager Countess Downe was extremely generous toward him and he received invitations to stay over at her home at Baldersby Park. However, her ladyship was also dictatorial in church matters and, although previous incumbents had gone along with her wishes, Sabine refused to kowtow to her.

During his first year at Dalton, Sabine assembled a collection of obscure ancient poems under the title *Silver Store* and dedicated them to Lady Downe. Either by accident or design, some of the poems referred to dictatorial women and this slight appears not to have gone unnoticed. Sabine had made a grave mistake and was to regret it!

Only a few miles from Dalton is the historic market town of Knaresborough, known for its association with several unusual characters. One was John *Blind Jack* Metcalf, who despite his disability, became a military musician, rode with the hunt and ran off with another man's bride on the eve of the wedding. Metcalf became a successful builder of bridges and roads and was responsible for constructing the main road adjacent to the Brig Mission. Sabine features Metcalf in *Yorkshire Oddities Incidents and Strange Events*.

St Robert of Knaresborough was another notable man and Sabine comments in *Lives of the Saints* that, although Robert achieved sainthood within twenty years of his death, he was never actually canonised! St Robert's infamous riverside cave [a mile from the chapel] was also the scene of the grisly murder of Eugene Aram in 1745 and Sabine refers to this in his *Cliff Castles and Cave Dwellings of Europe*. Although the prophetess, Mother Shipton, is currently the most popular character associated with Knaresborough, Sabine surprisingly makes no reference to her.

Over the winter of 1868-9 Grace spent many hours knitting by the fireside and on 20th April 1869 gave birth to her first child, Mary. When Grace walked out with her child the local women followed tradition by pushing silver coins into the baby's hand and pinning items of egg, salt, white bread and matches to her clothes! Grace was astonished by this and when she told Sabine he ascertained that the egg brought the promise of immortality, the salt signified salubrity of mind and body, white bread promised things needed in this life and matches were to light the way to heaven in the next life.

Within the year Grace was pregnant again when her young life was put in grave danger. One evening she was brushing her hair in front of the dressing table mirror when a gunshot rang out of the darkness and a bullet smashed the bedroom window showering her head with glass. Upon hearing the shot, Sabine rushed out into the garden, but the felon had made good his escape.

A police investigation revealed that the intended victim was not Grace but their very pretty servant girl, who had treated a suitor's advances with such contempt that he had lain in wait in the garden with the intention of shooting her! The young man came from an adjoining farm and quickly left the area never to return.

In early August 1870 Edward visited his family by way of nearby Ilkley, where Sabine later featured the Moor and its cups and rings in *Strange Survivals & Superstitions*. Edward only stayed at Dalton for a few days and shortly after he left, Grace gave birth to another daughter, Margaret (Daisy). Her arrival created acute accommodation problems and, when Sabine appealed to Lord Downe for the house to be extended, he was refused. Sabine knew the reason why!

Meanwhile, Joseph Taylor informed Grace that he was to marry Miss Bessie Berry. Father Sharp conducted the ceremony on Christmas day 1870, when Grace and Sabine are believed to have been present. Joseph and Bessie lived at 1, Clubhouses Yard, Horbury [the site of the former police office] along with four of Joseph's children.

By the end of January 1871 living conditions at Dalton were so unbearable for Sabine that he contemplated sleeping in a caravan in the garden. Then, quite unexpectedly, he received the offer of the Crown Living at East Mersea, Essex. The offer came directly from the Prime Minister, Mr Gladstone, who was aware of Sabine's reputation as a hymn writer and had been taking a close interest in his latest work on *the Origin and Development of Religious Belief*. Sabine gratefully accepted the offer and left immediately for Essex with his family.

Chapter 9

Developing Interests

Writing was always high on Sabine's agenda, his main themes being history, mystery, religion, folklore and travel. When he left Yorkshire in 1871, he had almost ninety articles, books and a handful of hymns to his credit.

During seven years in the county, (three years at Horbury and four at Dalton), Sabine had revelled in the richness of the local culture and he left with sufficient material to produce two books.

The first was *Yorkshire Oddities and Strange Events* and in the preface Sabine uncharacteristically expresses his thoughts and feelings:

A residence of many years in Yorkshire, and an inveterate habit of collecting all kinds of odd and out-of-the-way information concerning men and matters, furnished me, when I left Yorkshire in 1872 with a large amount of material, collected in that county, relating to its eccentric children. A friend, when he heard that I was collecting such material, exclaimed, 'What are you about? Every other Yorkshireman is a character!' Such is the case. No other county produces so much originality, which when carried to excess, is eccentricity.

I look back with the greatest pleasure to the kindness and hospitality I met with in Yorkshire, where I spent some of the happiest years of my life. I venture to offer this collection of memoirs of odd people, and narrative of strange events, as a humble contribution to the annals of the greatest, not perhaps only in extent, of our English counties, and a slight return for the pleasant welcome it afforded a migratory penman from the South.

This collection of unusual tales features many interesting characters like Prophet Wroe of the Christian Israelite Sect who lived near Wakefield, James Naylor the Quaker, Blind Jack of Knaresborough and David Turton a Horbury musician.

An amusing tale included in the book and from Sabine's time in Horbury relates to a butcher who took his bride on honeymoon to Bolton Abbey in the Yorkshire Dales. When they returned home the man put his wife on the weighing scale and divided her weight into the cost of the wedding tour. After a quick calculation he exclaimed:

Eh! Lass thous't cost me fourteen pence ha'penny, a pound. Thous't dearest piece o'meat I iver bought!

To avoid embarrassment Sabine did not reveal the butcher's name until fifty years later when he published his Reminiscences. The butcher's name was James Walker [44] and his great grandson Paul Walker and mother Doreen continue to trade in the town. Both are able to recall a wealth of amusing tales that have been passed down through the Walker family.

Although Sabine first published *Yorkshire Oddities and Strange Events* in 1874, when the seventh edition appeared in 1987 it quickly became a regional best seller and is still in demand.

The second book was the previously mentioned situational novel entitled *The Pennycomequicks* in which Sabine thinly disguises Horbury as Murgatroyd - the maiden name of Richard Poppleton's wife. The main characters also have local names such as Mitchell, Cusworth and Sidebottom – pronounced Siddy-bot-tome - suggesting a hint of snobbery.

The plot is set around the lives of the Yorkshire wool barons and Sabine satirises them for selling serge cloth to both sides in the Franco-German war of 1871-2. He writes: *What is a man's loss is another man's gain! The rattle of guns in France produced the rattle of looms in Yorkshire; and every bullet put through a Frenchman's or a German's uniform put a sovereign into the pocket of a cloth weaver in England.*

In this novel Sabine briefly refers to the embarrassment he felt after writing *Through Flood and Flame* and repeats his deep-rooted grudge against the Horse & Jockey Public House when he describes it being washed away again, by the raging River Calder!

The writing of sermons also appealed to Sabine and he churned them out by the hundred. Although some were in leaflet form, many were in books such as: *One hundred Sermons for Extempore Preachers, The Preacher's Pocket, The Sunday Round and Sermons to Children.*

He also produced three volumes of *Village Preaching for a Year* dedicated *with love and veneration to Rev. John Sharp, M.A. Vicar of Horbury.* Sabine delivered one of the sermons from this book at St Michael's Church, Wakefield in 1870. It is entitled *Organisation* and he appended a footnote: *This sermon is not adapted to an ordinary country congregation. It was preached in a town church to an educated congregation but the subject is capable of simplification to the level of humble understanding* - Praise indeed for the congregation of St Michael's Church, whom Sabine obviously regarded as educated.

The value of Sabine's contribution to both sermons and music is evident from the fact that years later he received a commission to produce the official souvenir booklets for the coronations of Edward V11 and George V.

In common with many Victorian gentlemen, Sabine could draw and paint. As a young boy he was encouraged by his aunt Emily to experiment with paints in her studio and his father taught him by example. On his fourteenth birthday he received a copy of Rowe's Perambulation of Dartmoor from his Uncle, Thomas Bond, and said of the book: *It arrested my attention, engaged my imagination and was to me almost like a bible. When I obtained a holiday from my books, I mounted my pony and made for the moor. I rode over it, round it, put up at little inns, talked with the moormen, listened to their tales and songs in the evenings and during the day sketched and planned the relics that I then fondly supposed was connected with the druids.*

The detailed workmanship of church furniture particularly suited Sabine's small scale and intricate style and, although he tended to romanticise his topographical watercolours they are generally technically competent and well above average.

In 1865 Sabine was invited to be a judge at the Wakefield Industrial and Fine Art Exhibition [45] in a section on Stationery, Printing, Bookbinding and Penmanship. He also entered twelve of his Icelandic paintings in a section for Drawing, Paintings and Sculptures, for which he was awarded a 1st Class medal. Further examples of his artwork are reproduced in *Strange Survivals* & Superstitions, *A book of Dartmoor, Deserts of Southern France* and C*liff Castles and Cave Dwellings of Europe.*

In 1868 Sabine donated a choice collection of his watercolours from Iceland and Switzerland to Gatrill who was raising funds to build a Mission House at the Brig. However, it is not known who purchased these paintings or how much money they raised. His painting of Pentelstein is believed to be from the same series. When six of Sabine's paintings of other European scenes were sold at auction in 1996, they raised between £350 & £750 each.

Sabine also collected paintings with a religious theme. The artists were generally little known continental artists such as Lavidiere, Cornelius Engebright, Paul Deschwanden and Edward Tyck. Sabine invited Tyck, who was from a new school of artists, to visit him at East Mersea and when he took up the offer, he

41. Le Defille Des Anglais by S. Baring-Gould.

42. *Watercolour painting of Pentelstein by S. Baring-Gould.*

and Gatrill showed him around. They visited London and Windsor, where Tyck was actually stunned by the lack of imagination on the part of English architects.

He also told his hosts that one evening he was working 6 feet down inside a vault in Bruges cemetery copying religious frescoes when, from the twilight above, he overheard two Germans conversing about skeletons:

'Ach! Gott im Himmel. Here is another. I wonder if we peered in whether we would be so fortunate as to see the skeleton?'

'Bah Rosalie! One skeleton is like another' came the reply.

As the visitors peered down into the vault the light was cut off which prompted Tyck to shout,

'From the depths I have called to you. Oh Lord hear my voice'

'Blimey!' shouted the man and they ran off abandoning their umbrella.

When the woman looked back and saw Tyck climbing out of the tomb she ran off towards the town shouting 'Run darling. Run!'

As an antiquarian, Sabine saw the unnecessary removal of artefacts as pure vandalism and in his case this applied particularly to church pew ends, pulpits and rood screens. He went out of his way to conserve such items, not only at Lew but elsewhere.

During a visit to Kenton Church, Devon, Sabine was alarmed to see that the old pulpit had been *restored* out of existence. He immediately searched out the original panels, consulted his boyhood drawings and arranged for the original pulpit to be restored to its former glory! Such work required considerable expertise and Sabine engaged his cousin, Bligh Bond, [46] a Bristol architect and specialist advisor on church restoration programmes to undertake such works.

The simple beauty of plants was always a joy to Sabine and, when only eight years old, he noted the profusion of beautiful primula and anemone growing in the snow as the family coach trundled over the Simplon Pass into Italy. As a teenager he wrote to his Uncle Thomas Bond, describing the behaviour of the continental ferns and heathers and commenting on a marked reduction in the number of scarlet anemone, saxifraga, pyramydalis and gentians!

In later life Sabine was so struck by the beautiful autumnal colours of the Black Forest that he immediately placed an order for 600 Bird Cherry Carmine trees which were planted in the woods of his estate. Unfortunately this impulsive project proved an expensive failure because the saplings failed to prosper, giving greater satisfaction to the birds than to Sabine!

His favourite flower was the delicate harebell and, although it has never grown well in the West Country, Sabine often pondered whether it would flourish on his grave, its little bells dancing in the wind to lull him in his last sleep. Alas, his burial vault did not permit this!

One of Sabine's fellow judges and exhibitors at the Wakefield Exhibition was

43. The old pulpit at Kenton Church, Devon.

44. The 'restored' pulpit at Kenton Church that was removed and replaced by the old one.

Thomas Gissing, a dispensing chemist of Westgate, Wakefield and writer of botanical books [47]. In his spare time Gissing went grubbing [searching] for specimens of plants in hedge bottoms and was often accompanied by his son, George Gissing (1857-1903), [48] who was destined to become a prominent Victorian writer and man of letters

When Sabine lectured at Wakefield Mechanics Institute he met Thomas again and they became friends through their mutual interest in botany. Sabine soon moved away to Dalton but when he discovered the profusion of wild orchids and forget-me-nots there he wrote to Thomas Gissing about his findings:

8th June 1869.
Dear Mr Gissing,
    I send you some of the bulbs of the Orchis. My wife and I went out with a trowel and basket last night and dug them up. Are you sure that the yellow flower is a Barbaro/ea, it grew wild in a cornfield, and I transplanted it to my garden where it is very showy. I enclose a leaf. I think I did not send one in my note.
    A bright blue gentian grows here & blooms at the close of summer. If you can spare a few days for botanising & like to make my house a centre I shall be delighted to see you. Pillmoor[sic] [49] is famous for its flowers. The great swampy flat is being fast enclosed I am sorry to say. My station is Sessay N.E.R. next to Pillmoor Station.
    Believe me to remain,
    Yours truly, S. Baring-Gould. [50]

It is not clear whether Gissing ever took up Sabine's invitation to visit Dalton, but their friendship came to an unfortunate end when Gissing died suddenly in 1870 at the age of forty-one. His widow, Margaret, was forced to sell the house and business and she moved into nearby Stamp Office Yard with her five young children.

    In due course young George Gissing gained a place at Owens College, the forerunner to the University of Manchester.

45. Thomas Waller Gissing (1829-1870).

46. George Robert Gissing (1857-1903).

Wakefield Industrial & Fine Art Exhibition, 1865.

LITHOGRAPHED EXPRESSLY FOR THE OFFICIAL CATALOGUE BY ALFRED GREEN, DEWSBURY.

47. The Wakefield Industrial and Fine Art Exhibition of 1865 was held in the building with the flag, where the Town Hall now stands. The Mechanics Institute where Baring-Gould lectured is on the left.

George excelled there until he was expelled for a theft connected with his love of a young prostitute, Nell Harrison. This act of youthful indiscretion led to George being shipped off to America in 1876 to make a fresh start.

After taking a temporary teaching post at Boston's Waltham High School, George wrote for the Chicago Tribune but soon left for New York and then the City of Troy. Unable to settle, he moved to London where he married Nell in 1879 and commenced writing. In 1891 he moved to 1, St Leonard's Road, Exeter where he was heard to exclaim: *every morning when I wake I thank heaven for silence.* Gissing also referred to the Mount Radford area of Exeter as *a flowery and bowery little suburb of the Victorian bourgeoisie* [51]. While writing *Born in Exile (1891)* and *Denzil Quarrier (1891)* Gissing also wandered in the countryside by the River Exe.

When Gissing returned to London two years later, he wrote the *Private Papers of Henry Ryecroft (1902)* which contains references to his walks in the Devon countryside and a love of wild flowers. Writing mainly of the class-ridden society of his day, George focussed upon sex, money and exogamous marriages. His novel *Our Friend the Charlatan (1901)* [52] mirrors Sabine's exogamous marriage. It would be interesting to know if Sabine read it and more importantly, what he thought of it! George Bernard Shaw also showed an interest in such relationships and after meeting Grace during a visit to Lew Trenchard is said to have been inspired to create the character of Eliza Doolittle in *Pygmalion*!

Despite much adversity, George Gissing became a respected novelist and man of letters. It is ironic that when he died at the age of forty-six in 1903, he had never really had the opportunity to enjoy his success.

Although Sabine's letter to Thomas Gissing in 1869 appears to have been the last communication between them, there is a sequel. When George Gissing's diaries and letters (see Appendix D) were published in 1992, they contained several references to Sabine. Although mainly critical and rather snobbish, they confirm that George kept abreast of his literary efforts. There is no indication that Sabine and George ever met after they both left Yorkshire.

Chapter 10

A Decade in Essex

Mersea Island, Essex, is situated some ten miles from Colchester and access is via a causeway known as the Strood, which becomes impassable at high tide. The population of the Island in 1871 was around thirteen hundred divided into two parishes, East and West.

The West was the most heavily populated parish and a large, closely-knit community of fishermen lived in an area known as The City. The fishing boats were moored in the deep mud channels or beached on the hard and those no longer serviceable were used as homes. While the men-folk fished offshore, the women glided across the extensive mud flats on wooden skis collecting shellfish. During the season, oysters were dispatched to Scott's and Overton's Oyster Saloons in London's West End where their discerning clientele washed them down with Chablis or Guinness Stout.

In contrast, East Mersea is more rural and when Sabine arrived there on the 21st March 1871 his household consisted of himself, Grace, two year-old Mary and baby Margaret. He also employed three general servants: Violet Mary Jackson aged 18 years of Finchley, Charlotte Hughes aged 21 years from nearby Langenhoe and John Horner aged 12 years of Dalton. After the confines of the cottage at Dalton the large rectory at East Mersea was ideal for Sabine's growing family.

Within the week Sabine was inducted as rector of the church of St Edmund King & Martyr. One of his first duties was to meet a parish deputation requesting the restoration of the old village orchestra, which had been replaced by a harmonium. Sabine rejected the request but later regretted this because the sound of the harmonium, which he did not like, could not be improved, whereas there was always the possibility that an orchestra could!

During hot weather, life was made unbearable by mosquitoes that swarmed across the nearby mud banks, spreading a form of malaria known as ague, for which the only cure was to sit over a warm fire until it passed. Residents also had to contend with the smell of decomposing sprats and loads of stinking waste from the streets of London that was spread over the fields as fertiliser. This situation irritated Sabine's delicate

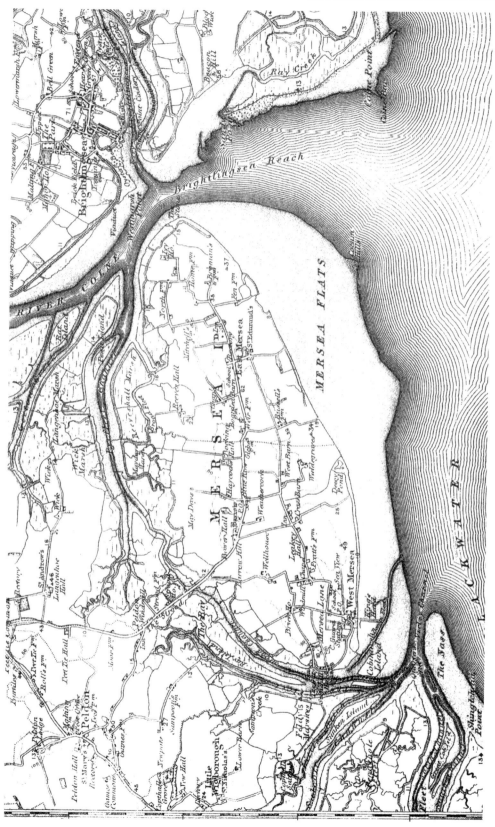

48 Mersea Island, Essex, in 1884.

health and, within three months of his arrival, he and Gatrill left for a tour of Belgium where they met the artist Edward Tyck.

That first summer Edward visited his son and family for a couple of weeks. The Rectory was in a poor state of repair and Edward experienced weird piping noises as the wind whistled through his bedroom. Sabine likened the sound to the souls of drowned sailors, sobbing all night from their watery grave, unable to reach the fire to thaw their chilled limbs and this prompted him to write a poem:

The Souls on the Wind.
The wind blows cold on waste and wold,
It bloweth night and day,
The souls go by twixt earth and sky
Incessant - know no stay.
They fly in clouds, and flap their shrouds
When full the moon doth sail.
At dead of night, when quenched all light
We hear them sigh and wail ....

The ceaseless easterly wind badly burned the children's faces and Grace had to consult the local doctor for advice. The recommended treatment proved both ineffective and expensive and, on the advice of her neighbour at East Mersea Hall, Grace applied glycerine ointment which cured the problem. As Edward left he awarded Sabine a generous income of four hundred pounds a year.

The parish was such a sleepy backwater that when Sabine mistakenly gave the same sermon two weeks running no one even noticed! With many spare hours between clerical appointments, Sabine began recording the history of his family in a large bible. Up to that time he had never known his exact date of birth and his father confirmed it as 28th January 1834.

Thereafter Sabine spent endless hours literally delving into parish chests and turning the dusty pages of old records to determine his antecedents. His painstaking research and letter writing eventually led him to the round room at the British Library where he rubbed shoulders with the literary luminaries of his day. The fruits of his painstaking research and family tree are deposited in Plymouth Library.

Sabine was desperate for a son and heir and in October 1871 he informed his father that Grace was expecting another child. He also commented that she had swallowed an egg of some monster newt or crocodile that had hatched and thriven within her! This strange remark appears to have been borne out of his research into salamanders for his *Book of Household Tales*. Sabine also informed his father that, in the absence of local friends, he had arranged for his sister, Margaret, and husband, Theodore (Marsh), to act as Godparents.

On 17th November 1871 Sabine wrote to his father: *I now have a son. He promises to be vigorous in health and stalwart in body. Grace produced a son and*

49. The church of St Edmund King & Martyr, East Mersea, Essex.

50 . The old vicarage, East Mersea, Essex.

heir and Grace is on the sofa by the fire and at her knitting, she is such an active little body that she cannot be kept from doing something.

This pregnancy took its toll on Grace who suffered a pro-lapsed womb and the doctor ordered her to rest. Having been referred to as a newt and crocodile by his father the child was fortunate to receive the straightforward name of Edward Sabine!

Soon afterwards Sabine commenced *Lives of the Saints* and, although he found the work both monotonous and demanding, his effort was rewarded when an order was received for a thousand copies prior to publication. Over the next five years Sabine produced a fourteen-volume hagiography [lives and legends of saints] at an agreed price of £50 a copy. Unfortunately he never received full payment for this tremendous piece of work, because the publisher went bankrupt.

At Whitsuntide 1872 Sabine and his family visited his father in Devon en route to a holiday in France. They were never to see Edward again. While they were away they visited Rotterdam, Cologne and Wurzburg and sampled the fine Stein wine. Unfortunately the travelling caused Grace to tire quickly and when she suffered repeated nosebleeds Sabine, offered to cork and seal her nostrils with sealing wax. Grace obstinately refused!

On receiving news of his father's death, Sabine also learned that he had inherited Lew Trenchard Estate. It was quite a shock, because his father had always made it plain that by taking holy orders he would have to forgo it. The reason for this change of mind was probably connected with Willy's mental instability, the fact that Edward Drake was too young and of course in those days, Margaret did not come into the reckoning.

Although Sabine became the Squire of Lew Trenchard, he decided to remain at East Mersea in deference to his elderly Uncle Charles, who had been the Rector of St Peter's Church since 1833. Excepting an unsuccessful application to become a canon at Westminster, Sabine resigned himself to his living in Essex.

In January 1874 Beatrice Gracieuse was born and soon afterwards Sabine took Grace to London where he had hired a window to view the celebrations as the newly married Duke of Edinburgh entered the City. Sabine also visited Somerset House to work on the family tree and perhaps looked in on nearby Kings College which he had attended thirty years earlier.

On their return to Mersea Sabine commenced writing *Yorkshire Oddities*. Over the next six years the couple had four more children: Veronica (Vera 1875), Julian (1877), William (1878) and Barbara (1880). Fortunately, a new governess assisted Grace with her workload. Her name was Miss Biggs, an ex-schoolmistress who was a strong and loyal character. In addition to keeping the children under control, Miss Biggs played the church organ and acted as a companion for Grace. She remained with the family for many years. Her presence at East Mersea enabled Grace to take an interest in the welfare of local children who were mainly uncouth and ran around in cut down ex-military uniforms.

In those days Sabine described the islanders as shy, suspicious and dull and his only contact with educated minds was with a solicitor named Keeling of Colchester, who later visited him at Lew Trenchard, and the Reverend Pertwee who lived across the Colne estuary at Brightlingsea. However, visits to Pertwee were dictated by the vagaries of tide and weather, and involved a long walk, a pick-a-back through the mud and being rowed in an open ferryboat across the estuary. Once there, it was not unusual for Pertwee to have been called away!

During the summer months Sabine and Grace often visited Mr Baker, the ferryman, and his wife for tea and shrimps. The Bakers were popular local characters and lived in an upturned hulk beside the estuary of the River Colne. Mrs Baker enjoyed a tipple and visitors were greatly amused when her husband threw a bucket of cold water over his wife's head to sober her up. As a shareholder in the Colchester Brewery Company Sabine probably found the situation doubly amusing!

While Sabine was in Essex the death occurred of the Reverend Robert Stephen Hawker M.A. (1805-1875) who was one of The South West's most colourful characters and the Vicar of Morwenstowe. His parish was in a remote coastal area of North Cornwall and, when local wreckers lured ships onto the rocks, he ministered at the funerals of those poor souls who drowned.

Like Sabine, Hawker was a well educated, but eccentric, man and it was he who introduced the harvest festival into the church calendar. He also wore a poncho on his daily rounds, carried a pet pig and excommunicated his cat for catching a mouse on a Sunday. Some were never sure who was the greater romancer, Hawker or Baring-Gould!

When Hawker died several biographers engaged in an unholy rush to publish the story of his remarkable life, and not to be outdone, Sabine published *The Vicar of Morwenstowe* in great haste. In so doing he made a number of errors for which he was strongly criticised by Hawker's young widow. Although subsequent reprints were amended, the furore merely served to increase the appeal of Sabine's book. However, Sabine also suffered a backlash, because his critics never allowed him to forget the errors.

Around 1879 Sabine began work on a melodramatic novel set on the marshes around Mersea Island. The title was *Mehalah* and the eponymous heroine was a wild young woman created around the character of Mrs Baker, the ferrywoman. Sabine also cast the brooding villain of the piece, one Elijah Rebow, in the mould of a local leading dissenter!

The author, Algernon Charles Swinburne (1837-1909), compared this novel with Emily Bronte's *Wuthering Heights* and commented that Elijah Rebow bore a strong resemblance to Heathcliffe. Although Sabine accepted the comparison he was adamant that the plot came to him during a sleepless night. Some believe that this powerful, impulsive and bitter story was a reflection of Sabine's unhappy association with Mersea Island. [A note in Sabine's diary confirms that he was depressed when he wrote Mehalah].

Mehalah epitomises the power of Baring-Gould's observation and his ability to blend fact with fiction. To cross the Strood from Mersea and follow the trail of Mehalah through the pathways of Ray Island, visit the ruined church at Virley where Sabine 'married' Mehalah to Elijah Rebow and visit the same Rose Inn at Peldon all seems so real even though it was written well over a century ago.

Working continuously on *Lives of the Saints* affected Sabine's health and in the summer of 1874 he and Gatrill left for Eifel in Germany. Their itinerary included visits to churches and in particular the mineral mine of Daun. This mine had been responsible for the downfall of Sabine's grandfather's manganese mine at Lew that once had an annual yield of 10,000 tons. The workings and spoil heaps remain at Lew Trenchard to this day.

At Munster Maifield Sabine and Gatrill visited a bar to quench their thirsts and at some point Sabine was mistakenly identified as an outlawed Jesuit priest. He didn't stop to argue and he and Gatrill made a dash for the safety of the Moselle, from where they returned home.

The following summer, Sabine suffered from rheumatism and joined Gatrill and two clergy friends from Horbury and Wakefield on a month's trip to the Algau Alps. They visited Strasburg and Cologne, but while bathing one of the men (possibly the Reverend William Highway Kirby) was attacked by mosquitoes. The poor fellow became so ill that Gatrill cut short his holiday to escort him home.

During Sabine's sojourns Grace had to deal with any business matters or problems as she saw fit. While he was away she occupied herself by writing regularly to her father

51 St Peter's Church, Lew Trenchard.

Erratum: the above church is St Paul de Leon, Staverton.

and sisters. During the time they lived in Essex her step-mother Bessie had four daughters, Elizabeth (1871), Emma (1873), Ellen (1874) and Alice (1876). In total her father Joseph raised thirteen children from his two marriages and every Christmas Grace sent a few shillings to be shared among them.

One day Mrs Baker told Grace that the previous evening the crew of a rowing boat off East Mersea claimed to have seen mermaids swimming in the moonlit sea. Realising that she and a lady friend had been bathing there around that time, Grace said it must have been them and gave the matter no more thought. Shortly afterwards she was informed that it could not possibly have been her - because the mermaids had fish tails and scales - a matter that the boat crew could swear to!

In 1876 Sabine received an appeal from his Uncle Charles, who was very concerned at the behaviour of the tenant of Lew House and the conduct of the licensee of the Blue Lion Public House - also part of the estate. Leaving Gatrill in charge at East Mersea, Sabine took his family to Devon to investigate. The outcome was that Sabine gave the elderly tenant and his young flirtatious wife notice to quit and dismissed the libertine licensee of the Blue Lion, who had seduced the wife of the local saddler.

Having shown his mettle, Sabine decided to remain in Devon and continued with the restoration of the church pews. However, the family was devastated when three-year old Beatrice died suddenly from whooping cough. After the funeral, they returned to East Mersea and Lew House was re-let. Sabine also commissioned a marble statuette of Beatrice modelled on her elder sister Vera. It was installed at the rear of the pulpit in St Peter's Church and depicts Beatrice with the liquid of life spilling out of her favourite drinking mug that had been given to her by Susan Pengelly, the coachman's wife. The mug was inscribed with the words *Think of Me*.

That September Grace was in the latter stages of another pregnancy, when news arrived from the Vicar of Staverton, Devon, that the 17th century remains of the Gould family were to be cleared out of the church. Sabine immediately went there and saw the skull of Julian Rowe (1636-96) a female ancestor whose will he had recently read while researching his family history at Somerset House. While Sabine was holding Julian's skull and pondering what kind of person she had been in life, he received news that Grace had given birth to a son. He promptly named the boy Julian.

The remains of fourteen Gould ancestors were transported to St Peter's Church Lew Trenchard for re-interment and Sabine had several of the stone tablets secured on the church walls. This somewhat unusual occurrence was not well received in the parish.

In 1880 Sabine acquired a pair of chandeliers from St Jacques Church, Malines, France. He presented one of them to the Church of St Paul De Leon, Staverton and had the other installed in his own church from where it was stolen a century later. In 1891 Sabine returned to Staverton Church to attend the dedication of the restoration of the intricate 15th century rood screen undertaken by Bligh Bond. It is noteworthy that Robert S. Hawker also had links with the same church.

Shortly after Julian's birth all the family caught ague, so Sabine took them to Freiburg to recuperate, once again leaving Gatrill in charge.

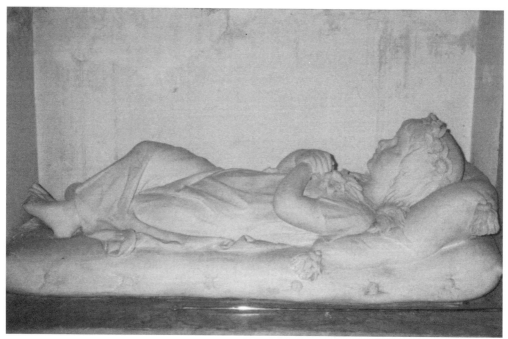

52. Memorial to Beatrice Gracieuse Baring-Gould, St Peter's Church, Lew Trenchard.

The next event of note was the death of Sabine's forty-four year-old brother, Willy, at Witham in Essex. As a young man he been a civil engineer and worked on a bridge in the U.S.A. and on a large railway contract near Doncaster, Yorkshire. After years of mental anguish he died while in hospital and was buried in East Mersea churchyard in February 1880.

The third brother, Edward Drake, worked in Brazil where he contracted yellow fever. On the journey home in 1887 he was involved in a shipwreck and died after spending two nights in an open boat. He was 37 years old. Sabine was of the opinion that the health of his two brothers broke down because Edward their father had pressured them into occupations for which they had no real ability.

Sabine's sister Margaret (Sissy) married Theodore Henry Marsh who spent fifty years as the rector of Cawston, Norfolk. Following a family tragedy the couple adopted a young nephew also named Theodore, who followed his uncle into the church and later took over his living.

The death of Sabine's uncle, the Reverend Charles Baring-Gould, in February 1881 heralded Sabine's departure from Mersea. He was pleased to be returning to his native Devon where he could settle at last with his wife and growing family of seven children. During his ten years on Mersea he wrote almost sixty titles including best-seller *Mehalah* which is still in popular demand.

Chapter 11

Life at Lew Trenchard

When Sabine arrived at Lew Trenchard in 1881 he knew that a lot of effort was required to bring it up to standard. He had already considered offering the church living to Gatrill so that he could concentrate on the role of squire. However, knowing that with the love of the people and by the grace of God things always worked out for the best, he decided to embrace both roles. By so doing he joined that rare breed of men known as squarsons [squire & parson].

With Lew House still occupied by a tenant, Sabine commenced modernising the rectory, formerly occupied by his uncle Charles. It was the end of June before the work was complete and Grace arrived with the children.

On 19th July 1881 Sabine presented himself to his own living and was installed rector by the Bishop of Exeter. He immediately began implementing the three objectives formulated when he was a young man:

To:

• Restore the Parish Church

• Improve the morals and spirituality of the people of the Parish.

• Renovate and extend Lew House.

Although Sabine quickly made his presence felt within the parish, he had little respect for the church hierarchy and, as a consequence, his name featured prominently in the bishop's black book! With his forthright views he was something of a loose cannon and was left very much to his own devices, which appears to have suited him.

The church of St Peter, Lew Trenchard had been founded by St Petrock around 560 A.D. and was re-dedicated to St Peter in 1261. Sabine had begun work on the church pews while still living at Mersea and when funds became available he improved the fabric of the building, installed memorial windows, chandelier lighting and acquired religious paintings.

The huge wooden rood screen in the church was restored by Bligh Bond who engaged the Misses Pinwell to execute the carvings and Sabine's daughter Margaret to paint the decorative panels. Other improvements included the pulpit in the gift of H.M. Sperling, re-constructed clergy stalls and an eagle lectern from Brittany. To this day St Peter's Church is said to be a perfect expression of Sabine's taste, personality and devotion.

As Rector, Sabine chose to wear the traditional dress of a country parson consisting of a black wide brimmed hat, white dog collar, black jacket, waistcoat, trousers and boots. During his daily rounds he breezed straight into parishioner's homes at an early hour, whether they were ready to receive him or not! After parish rounds, Sabine usually returned home for breakfast and attended to any business matters before withdrawing into the library to write.

With the farming industry in the doldrums and a half-year return of only two pounds from the estate, Sabine's third objective of improving Lew House presented him with some serious financial difficulties. In the short-term he negotiated a loan of a thousand pounds at 3% interest from his Aunt Fanny and saved a similar sum by sending the children to be educated abroad.

However, when Sabine received a hundred pounds for three months work on *Mehalah,* he realised that writing novels was the way ahead and followed up with *John Herring* and *Margery of Quether*. As the money slowly began to come in Sabine planned an ambitious building and refurbishment programme.

Being the patron of his own living, Sabine appointed the curates, who all appear to have served him well. However, his suggestions for future deployment were not always heeded and when he recommended that his half-brother, Arthur should remain in Devon where his talents were best suited, the advice was ignored and he was appointed to St Martins, Haverfordwest. Fortunately, the move worked to Arthur's advantage because he was highly regarded there and became the Rural Dean of Roose.

Several of Sabine's other curates also made good progress within the church, including the Reverend Gilbert Arundell, who was his last curate and succeeded Sabine in 1924. The family connection was restored again in 1946 on the appointment of Guy F. Newman, who married Sabine's granddaughter, Eulalia. Newman was succeeded by Sabine's grandson, Bickford Dickinson, in 1961. The present vicar is Reverend John Heath who has responsibility for the United Benefice of Lifton, Broadwoodwiger, Stowford, Lewtrenchard with Thrushelton & Kelly with Bradstone.

In August 1882, when the three eldest Baring-Gould children returned home from school in Germany Sabine wrote in his dairy:

Mary, Margaret and Edward now returned from Freiburg where they have been at school for 10 months. Mary very white and tall. Edward thin and well, Margaret seems to have suffered least. It is as well they are home as they might have become seriously out of health by a longer stay. Mary particularly. German food does not suit English growing children.

It is clear from their manners that the two girls have been well cared for and that the tone of the school is good, honourable and refined. Dear Mary is as sweet as ever. Margaret is funny and natural. Sabine (Edward) has lost some of his freckles and has the same honest truthful look in his brown eyes and his heart is as warm as ever, dear fellow.

As a boy Sabine had been subjected to many dubious medical remedies and he took a great interest in the use of homeopathic recipes, charms and related superstitions. Although having no time for quacks, he valued the knowledge of the old village herbalists, once so common in rural areas. One such person was an elderly widow named Marianne, who lived in a broken down old house at Lew. Her extensive knowledge of herbs and charms intrigued Sabine who once sampled a glass of her powerful metheglin mead and became so tipsy that he fell off his pony on the way home!

These are typical examples of a recipe and a charm:

A cure for jaundice.

Take an old well-blackened clay tobacco pipe.
Grind up the bowl, take as much as will go on a sixpence, before each meal.

A verbal charm for a sprain.

As Christ was riding over Crolly Bridge, His horse slid and sprained its leg. He alighted and spoke these words. 'Bone to bone, and sinew to sinew.' And He blessed it and it became well. And so shall (persons name) *come well, in the Name of the Father, and the Son, and of the Holy Ghost.* (To be repeated three times).

Marianne was also familiar with the mysterious powers of the poisonous plant mandrake (atropa mandragora) with a root that resembles the shape of the human body and shrieks [squeaks] when plucked from the ground. Sabine tried his best to get Marianne to part with her knowledge of this plant, but she steadfastly refused and took the secret to the grave with her. Not to be beaten, Sabine researched the properties of this strange plant and refers to it in Further Reminiscences [53].

Sabine knew from experience that superstition had far more vitality in people's minds than religion and as a clergyman this must have been a very bitter pill for him to swallow. Even Susan Pengelly, the wife of his coachman, believed that Beatrice's life could have been saved by cutting some hair from the cross on the back of an ass and placing it in a silk bag around her neck!

In April 1882 Sabine was appointed a county magistrate and sat at Lifton Petty Sessions with other worthies such as Col Byng, H. S. Sperling and P.D. Rowe. The police also regularly attended Lew House to swear out warrants. At that time felons plagued much of rural Devon and Sabine relied on two large dogs to deter unwelcome visitors.

Sabine had grand plans to form a large lake in the nearby slate quarry and in 1883 Grace cut the turf to divert the garden stream into the quarry.

The following year Sabine learned that a large earthquake had struck Mersea Island causing extensive damage to both parish churches and the old vicarage. Fortunately there were no fatalities.

In 1885 Sabine and Gatrill re-visited the medieval, fortified town of Feldkirch in Austria to see the fine display of alpine plants in the botanical gardens. As they travelled through Schruns, Sabine saw the fine dark haired women working in the fields harvesting cabbage to make sauerkraut and suddenly exclaimed, *they have grown busts!* He had learned on a previous visit that as a matter of delicacy and fashion, the women had suppressed their breasts by lacing them down with a wooden board across their chest in order to look like men.

After calling at Innsbruck, the two friends travelled to Paris where Sabine officiated at the marriage of his American cousin, Alex Baring, to Miss Louise King Thorne in the British Embassy Chapel. Alex was the son of Sabine's great-uncle, Charles Baring, who had an estate at Flatrock, South Carolina. When Sabine's father, Edward, had visited him in 1830, he had described Charles as a charming man, of sweet temper and old English courtly ways. During the American Civil War Alex was sent over to England and Edward enrolled him in the British Navy. After his marriage Alex went sheep farming in Nevada and then into business in New York with Oliver Northcote.

While Sabine was away, Lew House became vacant so Grace took the initiative and moved in. Sabine slipped into the garden un-noticed when he returned home and,

53. The Baring-Goulds on holiday at Bude.

on meeting Grace, told her she was really marvellous because of the way she had managed the move and adjusted everything, likening her to a general in the household. Shortly afterwards, Grace who was pregnant again, took the children on holiday to Bude, where they stayed in a small Elizabethan cottage. When they returned home a week later, they all looked really well.

The birth of their eleventh child, Henry, that year concentrated Sabine's mind on the lack of household accommodation.

After examining the options, Sabine decided to convert the rectangular shaped house into a fashionable E-shaped Jacobean style mansion by adding a protruding library and ballroom on the wings and a substantial porch between them.

54. Grace Baring-Gould with baby.

This ambitious programme disturbed almost every room in the house, revealed hidden fireplaces and unearthed coins from the reigns of Henry III and Charles I. When an old door from Sir Francis Drake's birthplace at Crowndale House became available, Sabine had it installed in the house. He also acquired a four-poster bed associated with Queen Henrietta (1609-1669) the wife of Charles 1.

The library on the east wing was built with large windows on three sides giving views over the glen, the dower house and the terrace. As Sabine stood writing at his high desk by the terrace window, he enjoyed the warmth and light of the sun and monitored the arrival of visitors. On the inner end of the library is a tablet bearing the motto of Crusader John Gold (circa 1217) *Toujours Sans Tache* - Always without stain that was loosely translated into *Gold Bydeth Ever Bright* which Sabine amended to *Gould Bydeth Ever Bright*.

He also worked on this unfinished poem:

55. Coat of arms of the Gould family

Gold makes not Gould, nor any loss
Turneth pure Gould to sorry dross
Silver that is gilded is not gold
Gold by sunlight bright however old
Trust not in gold, but in Gould is true
Gold is right good but....

During the alterations undertaken by his own team of masons, Sabine imported a substantial porch, bearing a sundial dated 1696. This had been removed from a Gould property at Staverton and was installed in the centre of the front of Lew House. The ballroom planned for the west wing was not a priority at that time, but Sabine also installed a circular, gravity-fed water fountain in front of the porch featuring an Alsation gooseherd, modelled on one he had seen in Labenwolf, Germany.

As more funds became available

56. Lew Trenchard House after conversion.

Sabine upgraded the c16 Dower House along with other properties on the estate. He also built a detached house by the flooded quarry known as Rampenstein (The Ramps) occupied by a Mrs Bussell, a pair of substantial semi-detached cottages at the junction of the road to Lew Down and a French-style dovecote at the rear of Lew House. When the quarry was filled, he also constructed an alpine style boathouse with a convoluted religious chronogram designed by Gatrill above the door. The boathouse was well used by family, friends and local children, who rafted and fished there.

Sabine and Grace received many visitors and guests and were renowned for their hospitality. Grace is said to have been very gracious, handling her responsibilities with great confidence and dignity. During one of Sabine's many absences, a German Judge once dropped in on her unannounced and although he spoke no English and she no German, she entertained him extremely well! When the Sunday Companion newspaper ran a series on *Wives of Famous Men* [54] they featured Grace. [Unfortunately the counties were wrongly quoted. Dorsetshire should have read Devonshire and Lancashire - Yorkshire!]

Despite many distractions, Sabine doggedly maintained an output of at least a chapter a day on his novels. He also received many commissions for specialist articles like a request to write a *History of Germany* for the *Story of the Nations Series* in 1886. His knowledge of that country was extensive and he produced at least four publications associated with it.

Although Sabine's income from writing was now quite considerable, as soon as money came it was quickly expended. The improvement of the estate and his large family were a huge drain on his income and he often checked the state of his finances at his bank in Tavistock before undertaking a new project.

THE WIVES OF FAMOUS MEN.

MRS. S. BARING-GOULD.

How little, as a rule, we know of the wives of famous men! Over-shadowed by the greatness of their husbands, we seldom hear of their existence. Yet how many famous men owe their strength and inspiration to the solicitude and encouragement of loving wives!

Let me introduce to the reader this week the wife of a man who has made himself famous in literature. There are few more perfect masters of fiction than the Rev. Sabine Baring-Gould, the rector of the quiet Dorsetshire village of Lew Trenchard. His wife is one of the most lovable women in the world—an ideal parson's wife. As Miss Grace Taylor, she was living a humble life in one of the Lancashire cotton-manu-facturing towns when she met her future husband. Struck by her beauty, and far more by her innate goodness, the Rev. S. Baring-Gould took her from the loom, and educated and married her.

57. The Wives of Famous Men
- Mrs S. Baring-Gould.

Chapter 12

Old Uncle Tom Cobley

and All

One evening in 1888, Sabine was invited to a dinner party at the home of his friend Daniel Radford who lived at Mary Tavy. During the evening, Sabine was persuaded of the need to collect the old folksongs before they were lost as the old singers died.

Although Sabine could locate the singers and collect the words without difficulty, he was not a musician and was unable to transcribe the tunes accurately without a piano so he had to invite the singers to Lew House. Sabine soon found this impractical and recruited two carefully chosen assistants.

The first was his friend, Henry Fleetwood Sheppard, who was Rector of Thurnscoe in South Yorkshire and the Precentor of Doncaster Choral Union. Sheppard, then aged sixty-three, was a publisher of church music and had a particular flair for ballads and dainty harmony as well as being an authority on the Noels and Carols of Flanders.

The second was Frederick W. Bussell of Brasenose College, Oxford. A doctor of both music and

58. Reverend H.F. Sheppard M.A. (1824-1901)

59. Reverend Dr F.W. Bussell D.Mus. D.D. (1862-1944).

theology, he once boasted of writing a million words in 18 months. Frederick was a dandy, with a high falsetto voice, who always wore a buttonhole to match his tie. Out of term he lived at The Ramps with his mother whom Sabine jokingly referred to as Baroness Rampenstein of Lew Trenchard. Sabine was greatly amused when he learned that Mrs Bussell and Frederick had once travelled abroad using this fictitious title. Frederick subsequently became vice-principal of his college and was described as a brilliant and wayward personality [55].

Many of the old singers were illiterate and had little regard for parsons. What they thought of Sabine and his colleagues as they travelled along the West Country lanes in Bussell's custom built, high-sided, luxury coach in search of singers is probably unrepeatable! However, after a few drinks even the most reluctant singers were happy to perform their repertoires of traditional songs, once so popular in public houses, at harvest suppers and bell ringers' feasts.

The singers included Old James Parsons, a hedger of Lew Down, who visited Lew House several times. He sang many fine tunes such as *By Chance it Was* - passed down by his father, whose own vast repertoire of songs had earned him the title of the *singing machine*. On a visit to the British Museum, Sabine traced the words of this song to the time of James I, when it was known as *The Court of Apollo*. Other fine tunes were collected from Richard Hard, a crippled stonebreaker, and John Helmore, a miller, who were both residents of South Brent.

It was washday when Sabine and Frederick visited the singer, Sally Satterly, in her squatter's home at Huccaby, Dartmoor. After entering the house Bussell inconsiderately ensconced himself on the copper boiler, so Sally did no more than set it alight to drive him off! As Sally went about her work she obligingly broke into song with the air *The Loyal Lover* and took great delight in having young Frederick follow her around taking down the tune.

One New Year's Eve Sabine and Frederick visited the Saracen's Head on Dartmoor, where they collected additional verses to that well-known tune, *Barbara*

97

Allen. On another occasion Sabine and Sheppard recorded the coarse words of *the Bold Dragoon* from Moses Cleve at Huccaby Bridge. While returning home over Dartmoor, they were drenched to the skin and took shelter at the home of Daniel Radford, who entertained them to lunch. As the two vicars stood drying themselves in front of the open fire, with their clerical coat tails gathered over their arms, Radford maliciously called his wife to observe them and said they resembled a pair of peacocks with tails spread!

Another popular melody was *The Bonny Bunch of Roses,* a favourite fo'castle song sung by sailors in the 1850s and thought to be an anti-Jacobin song connected with Napoleon. The tune was so popular

60. *John Helmore, retired miller and old Devon singer.*

in Yorkshire that a public house at Silkstone Common near Barnsley was reputedly named after it. The link with Yorkshire is not clear, but the press gangs were active there and sailors probably brought the song home when returning from the sea. Coincidentally, this hostelry is only a few miles from Sheppard's former parish at Thurnscoe.

When Sabine published *Songs of the West* in 1889, it contained well over a hundred tunes and many were annotated with the singer's name and the circumstance of its collection. Several of the tunes came from the collection of Frank Kidson (1855-1926) of Yorkshire, with whom Sabine exchanged ballads and folklore material.

61. *Richard Hard, retired stonebreaker and old Devon singer.*

The most popular tune from *Songs of the West* was *Widdecombe Fair….* with Old Uncle Tom Cobley and all! The Saturday Review described the book as *a rich and varied collection of humour, pathos, grace and poetic fancy.*

Sabine regarded the collection of these songs as the principal achievement of his life and was extremely disappointed when follow-up concert tours of the West Country flopped because music hall had taken over. However, Sabine probably earned something from this work because he made donations to some of the old singers, who often died in abject poverty.

In 1894-5 Sabine and Sheppard published *A Garland of Country Song.* This was followed by eight volumes of the *English Minstrelsie.* When Sabine and Cecil J. Sharp (ex-Clare College) collaborated in 1906, they produced *English Folksongs for Schools* and this resulted in many generations of schoolchildren singing songs such as, *Wraggle Taggle Gipsies-O, Strawberry Fair and This Old Man.*

Many of the collected songs contained crude expressions and, like Robbie Burns and Sir Walter Scott before him, Sabine sanitised those likely to cause offence. *The Bold Dragoon* is one such tune. In some quarters Sabine was criticised for altering the words, but he had always made it clear that the tune was more important than the words. When he kindly deposited some original scripts in Plymouth City Library, he was further criticised in Exeter for not depositing the scripts there! Further manuscripts are also deposited in the Houghton Library at Harvard University, USA[56].

By 1889 Sabine was completely exhausted. He was suffering from another chest infection and went to Rome to recuperate. While there he was contacted by W.H. Allen the publishers, who requested his impressions of Provence and Languedoc that he wrote of *In Troubadour Land.*

During the summer of 1890 Sabine resumed work on *Lives of the Saints* but returned to Rome again over winter to research the Caesars of the Julian and Claudian Houses. His unusual findings were incorporated into *The Tragedy of the Caesars* and the Athenaeum Reviewer wrote: *It will in no sense disappoint the general reader... Mr Baring-Gould has presented his narrative in such a way as not to make one dull page.* Sabine dedicated this work to Grace on their Silver Wedding Anniversary. In it he quoted Proverbs 31 verses 10 & 11:

The praise of a virtuous woman.
verse 10 Who can find a virtuous woman? for her price is far above rubies.
verse 11 The heart of her husband doth safely trust in her, so that he shall have no need of spoil.

Shortly afterwards the *Yorkshire Notes & Queries Magazine* featured Sabine in *A Gallery of Yorkshire Authors,* justified on the grounds that he had spent some years in Yorkshire as a curate and written Yorkshire Oddities. As a true Devonian this gesture

CONTENTS.

❧ ❧ ❧

English Folk-songs for Schools.

62. *Contents of English Folk-Songs for Schools by Sabine Baring-Gould and Cecil J. Sharp.*

would have amused him.

In January 1891 *The Daily Graphic* commissioned Sabine to visit the mediaeval Duchy of Teck in the Black Forest area of West Germany to research an article for the forthcoming marriage of Princess Mary of Teck to the Duke of Clarence. Sabine's comprehensive, illustrated article filled a four-page spread in the newspaper [57].

On his way home Sabine prepared for his next novel *Cheap Jack Zita* by visiting

Ely near Cambridge where he appears to have consulted with local historian Claude Drewitt Kingdon, the colourful vicar of Prickwillow. This story of human passion is set in the Fen District at the time of the Littleport Riots in 1816. Once again the topography is well set and the plot is brought to life by strong characters with local names.

Throughout his time at Lew Trenchard, Sabine maintained a close interest in the history and archaeology of nearby Dartmoor and thought nothing of tramping scores of miles across the moors to visit remote sites of interest. After joining the Devon Association in 1878, the Dartmoor Exploration Committee, and the Royal Institution of Cornwall, he worked closely with Robert Burnard, Hansford Worth, Reverend Irving Anderson and others who became the foremost archaeological authorities in the South West.

When Sabine wrote the Dartmoor based novel *Guavas the Tinner* in 1895-6, he

63. Hut ruin at Trewortha, Bodmin Moor, Cornwall by S.B.G.

had clearly undertaken much empirical research. Guavas Eldad, the eponymous hero, was cast as a poor Cornish miner, who befriended the last wolf in England and became torn between two females, one beautiful and treacherous and the other simply true and loving. The plot bears similarities to his first novel *Through Flood and Flame* and has a touch of morality in that people should believe in God and not superstition. Sabine dedicated the novel to Robert Burnard, who would have fully appreciated the setting and the characters.

Although some regarded the team as a bunch of enthusiastic amateurs, in their day they were probably at the leading edge of archaeological methodology. Their excavation of Grimspound on Dartmoor determined that, although the early occupants of hut circles had slept on stone platforms and used hearths for a fire, a complete absence of pottery proved significant in dating their findings. When Sir Arthur Canon Doyle later visited the site and sat smoking his pipe in hut three, he is also believed to have been inspired to use it as Dr Watson's hiding place in *The Hound of the Baskervilles*. Conan Doyle wrote of the moor:

'It is a wonderful place, the moor,' said he, looking round over the undulating downs, the long green rollers, with crests of jagged granite foaming up into fantastic surges. 'You never tire of the moor. You cannot think the wonderful secrets which it contains. It is so vast, and so barren, and so mysterious.'

Sabine became president of both the Devon and Cornwall Associations and duly presented papers and lectured in support of the advancement of science, literature and art. He also acted as consultant to other organisations including the Welsh Cymmrodorian Society.

However, Sabine's detailed arrangements did not always go to plan and disaster

64. Baring-Gould at the entrance to Grimspound, Dartmoor,

almost struck on bonfire night 1891, when he accompanied Edward Thomas of the Ordnance Survey to the prehistoric site of Trewartha on Bodmin Moor, Cornwall. When the survey was complete they set out in the fading light for a favourite inn at Five Lanes, where a feast of roast duck awaited.

As the pair tramped across the empty moor, they became disorientated and separated and when Sabine suddenly sank up to his armpits in a stinking bog, his cries for help went unheard. He only managed to struggle free by placing his long stick horizontally across the bog and pressing down to break the suction. As he slowly extricated himself from the mire, Sabine lost his leather gaiters in the process and only reached firmer ground by writhing along the surface on his stomach like a lizard.

The pair looked a sorry sight as they staggered into the hostelry stinking of Red Mire bog, where only a few weeks earlier a complete herd of cattle had disappeared without trace! Afterwards Sabine commented *I have ever entertained a repungence to wobbly ground. I like to have firm soil under my feet, theologically, morally, socially and financially!*

65 Stall Moor Circle Dartmoor in April 1894. Left to right – S. Baring-Gould, J.B. Rowe, J.D. Pode and W.G. Gray (Meavy).

The following year Sabine published over twenty items including a situational novel set on the coast of North Cornwall entitled *In the Roar of the Sea*. The Saturday Review described it as *one of the best-imagined and most enthralling stories the author has produced. Through All the Changing Scenes of Life* was also set in the same area and Sabine based the story on the words of a hymn written by Tate and Brady in 1696.

One of Sabine's favourites stories in those days concerned a little girl at Sunday School, whose teacher asked her, *Who made your body?* The girl thought a while and replied, *Mother made my body. But Aunt made my skirt!* On the subject of children, those interested in Harry Potter may be surprised to learn that in 1891 Sabine also wrote an article for the Gentleman's Magazine entitled The Philosopher's Stone!

As Sabine aged, the damp Devon winters were taking an increasing toll upon his health and in the autumn of 1892 he left for Les Eyzies to gather material for three books. These were: *The Deserts of Central France, Cliff Castles and Dwellings of Europe* and the novel *Noemi*.

Early in 1893 Sabine proudly conducted the wedding ceremony of his eldest daughter, Mary, when she married Arscott Dickinson of Dunsland House, North Devon. A reception for two hundred and fifty guests was held at Lew House and the couple left for the French Riviera. Next day Sabine and Grace entertained the farmers and their wives for lunch, followed in the evening, by a dance for the young people of the village. With a further eight daughters to marry off, Sabine and Grace became adept at organising large and expensive wedding celebrations.

The following year William Pengelly, the coachman, died. He was seventy-eight and, having commenced employment with Sabine's grandfather at the age of seven, had spent the whole of his working life serving the family. Pengelly had been a faithful servant and a good friend to Sabine, who was saddened by his loss. He was buried in the churchyard at Lew Trenchard.

On 10th October 1894 *The Sketch* newspaper caricatured Sabine as a learned literary figure dressed as a country parson. The article referred to the variety and volume of his literary output and the popularity of his *Songs of the West*. Sabine also featured in A *Page of Confessions,* [58] in which well-known personalities were invited to answer ten questions. His curt responses were rather disappointing, but he did volunteer that reading was his favourite occupation, prehistoric research his favourite pastime and that he admired Shakespeare. Although non-committal about his favourite novelist, it is known that Sabine was influenced by Charles Dickens.

New Years Day 1895 was a very special occasion, when the whole Baring-Gould family had dinner together at Lew House. This opportunity never arose again, because the sons were sent to make their own way in the world at the earliest opportunity and most of them went to work or live overseas.

Sabine's diverse lifestyle was of great interest to the public and that September his friend, Gatrill,

66. How The Sketch newspaper portrayed Baring-Gould in 1894.

published an article in the *Sunday Magazine* entitled *The Reverend S. Baring-Gould at Home.* The article revealed that, although Sabine could not ignore the need to generate income by writing novels, his real passion was history and topography and that he hoped to write of every county in England.

Sabine explained that the writing of *Yorkshire Oddities, Troubadour Land, The Deserts of Southern France* and collecting *The Songs of Devon and Cornwall* had all been pleasurable experiences. He also said that before putting pen to paper he visited a locality to ensure the story was true to nature. His retentive memory and fair powers of observation also relieved him from keeping many notes or having to spend time re-writing.

67. Shawl crocheted by Grace Taylor for the Diamond Jubilee of Queen Victoria.

The article emphasised that it would be a mistake to suppose that Sabine's literary efforts militated in any way against his usefulness as a clergyman. At a moment's notice he could prove himself a most sympathising friend and trusty spiritual guide to those in need. His church was well attended and visitors travelled many miles to listen to his short, pithy sermons, each designed to teach one truth.

In conclusion, Grace referred to her husband's comprehensive collection of art and antiquities and confided that he was taking holidays on Dartmoor, where the bracing air strengthened his lungs and warded off bronchial attacks.

In 1895 Sabine published a score of titles along with a series of short articles for the *Sunday Magazine* describing the components of a church including *The Church Porch, The Gallery, The Belfry* and *The Pulpit.* In the latter article Sabine featured the ornate pulpit in St John's Church, New Briggate, Leeds, which is now administered by the Church Conservation Trust.

The article on the *The Belfry* also features Yorkshire churches where the devil's knell was tolled at midnight on Christmas Eve. Although the practice was discontinued sometime after Sabine left Horbury in 1867, it still continues at nearby Dewsbury Minster, where Sir Thomas De Soothill, the 18th century Lord of the Manor, used it to atone for his sin of murdering a servant boy in a fit of temper.

Sir Thomas instructed that every Christmas Eve, one stroke of the bell be tolled for each year since the birth of Christ. As each year goes by this accumulative legacy becomes more difficult because the last stroke of the bell must coincide exactly with the stroke of midnight!

The wide range of subjects covered by Sabine brought him into contact with many leading publishers: Bodley Head, Smith Elder, Hayes, Skeffington, SPCK, Chatto & Windus, Methuen, Blackie, W.H. Allen and several leading newspapers and magazines. In some cases he was paid on a sliding scale of between 10% & 15% on up to two thousand book sales. A new edition of Songs of The West in 1905 earned him 9d. a copy plus 12% of sales to America. Unfortunately, the volume of sales is not quoted. There were also occasions when Sabine had to seek legal redress for breach of copyright.

On Whit Tuesday 1896, twenty-one-year old Vera laid the foundation stone for the library at Lew House. This was the final stage of Sabine's plan to produce the present E-shaped profile. The ballroom seats 80 people and the interior panelled walls are modelled on those at Dunsland House. The magnificent fireplace, ornate plasterwork, chandelier lighting, organ, parquet flooring and furniture create a superb setting for a wide range of events.

Grace had also been busy during this period and for the Diamond Jubilee of Queen Victoria in 1897, she crocheted a large, cotton shawl to celebrate the occasion. This has been handed down through the family and was used only a few years ago at the wedding of Grace's great, great granddaughter, Belinda Bemrose, at Lew Trenchard.

As the nineteenth century came to a close, Canon Sharp had recently retired at Horbury because of ill health. He was eighty-nine years old and when he retired he moved into an annexe at the House of Mercy to be nursed by friends. Sabine was then sixty-six years old - an age when many men were worn out or had given up. In his case he had many active years ahead of him and was currently researching the activities of the Celts, whose influence had once extended down through the west of the country and across to France.

Chapter 13

A New Century Dawns

As the new century dawned, Sabine was heavily involved with the activities of the Devonshire Association and was working on publications featuring Dartmoor, North Wales and Brittany. In 1902 the Royal Institution of Cornwall presented Sabine with a prestigious Henwood Gold Medal in recognition of his work on the Celts.

Although life remained hectic and rewarding for Sabine, Grace was concerned about the number of coughs and chest complaints that he suffered, since the idea of strengthening his lungs on Dartmoor was clearly not working. The only real cure for him was the dry air of France, but he soon discovered that regular visits there disrupted his vocation and family life. In June 1903 Sabine was writing the novel *In Dewisland* when he received news that Canon John Sharp was very ill. He wrote the following letter to the *Ossett Observer:*

Lew Trenchard, N. Devon
9th June 1903
Dear Sir - I am grieved to hear that the long and useful life of Canon Sharp is drawing to a close. The years I spent with him, as a curate and in his house, were very happy. He was always sympathetic, courteous, and forbearing.

He was remarkably patient under opposition. When first he went to Horbury there was bitter opposition to him, but it all broke down. Some most hostile to him failed in business, and disappeared from the scene; others changed to respect him, and became his friends. There was a struggle against his getting rid of the pews and substituting open benches, but he managed to carry his point.

He gave me a free hand with the mission at Horbury Bridge; he always trusted the men he had to do with, and who worked under him, with the result that they had the utmost confidence in him.

His was an uneventful life, and the years I spent at Horbury, as far as he was concerned, were uneventful - one day passing like another. His forbearance extended to his kitchen. We curates at last complained that we were tired at supper with cold shape and rhubarb jam, which we had had for nine months without any change, night after night; and thus only was he stirred to ordering hot rice pudding on alternate evenings; he would not have noticed the monotony but for us.

I should never call him a striking preacher. His sermons were good, homely discourses, rather inclined to be long; there was no originality in them, but nevertheless, non-the-less likely to be helpful. To sum him up, I know no man who so fully answered to the description of Nathaniel, 'an Israelite indeed in whom there is no guile'

I remain, yours truly,
S.Baring-Gould.

The death of Canon Sharp on 10th June 1903 dominated the northern newspapers and glowing testimonials arrived from far and wide. Sabine appears not to have attended the funeral because his sister Margaret [Marsh] was very ill at the time. He managed to visit her in Norfolk a few days before she died.

Over the next three years Sabine visited Germany, took Grace on holiday to Pau and spent a year on location writing a book on an introduction to *The French Riviera.* Other books in this series include *The Cevennes, The Rhine and The Pyrenees.*

On 5th January 1906 the nation was shocked by the news that S. Baring-Gould had died aboard a steamer in South Africa. Obituary notices appeared in the press and the family were inundated with telegrams of sympathy. It was a terrible mistake. The deceased was actually his cousin Edward Baring-Gould and when the press rectified the error the telegrams changed to ones of congratulation!

This unfortunate incident delighted Sabine who, like Samuel Langhorne Clemens (Mark Twain) before him, was able to read his obituary in the morning papers and see what others genuinely thought of him! He commented afterwards: *I find I have more friends than I knew of, so that this little error has softened my heart and made me feel thankful that I have a wider circle that feel kindly towards me than the little ring of my own family.*

As a man who regarded travelling abroad as the norm, Sabine's only real indulgence was the acquisition of antiquarian items that caught his discerning eye. Drake's door and Queen Henrietta's bed have already been mentioned but he also collected furniture, paintings, books, clocks, military weapons and glassware.

When Sabine's granddaughter, Cicely (Image) Briggs, published *The Mana of Lew* in 1993, [59] she determined that Lew House and Church are built on leylines. She also discovered symbols of the ancient mystery schools [60] on Sabine's household furniture and, although he may have imported the items in all innocence, Image was not convinced of this. [He was not a Freemason]. Tragically, Image lost her life in a road accident in December 1994.

While the owners of many historic houses claim the presence of a resident ghost, Lew Manor has two! Both apparitions are friendly and have a strong affinity with the property. The first takes the form of a White Lady, associated with Susannah Gould, who died in her wedding gown on her way home from Lew church in 1729. A village legend says that seven parsons met under an ancient oak by the slate quarry to lay her ghost, but one was so drunk that the White Lady was conjured into the form of a white owl that was shot some time later!

The other was a midnight caller known as Old Madam, associated with Margaret Gould (1711 - 1795), who earned the eternal thanks of her descendants by safeguarding the estate from the reckless gambling habits of her son Edward, alias *The Scamp*.

Neither ghost has been seen for many years but James and Sue Murray, the present proprietors of Lew Trenchard Manor, report that one of the room doors that is always left unlocked is occasionally found locked without explanation! Sabine had a keen interest in such phenomena and published a book on ghosts in 1904 [61]. Although Edward had suppressed Sabine's interest in fairytales, this only made him more curious and over the years he amassed sufficient material to write at least twenty books relating to such matters. When Sabine was almost eighty years old, he wrote *A Book of Folklore* (1913) in which he relates the story of the ghosts of the White Lady and Old Madam.

68. Three of the Baring-Gould daughters: Cicely (Mrs Tinley), Joan (Mrs Priestley) and Grace (Mrs Calmady Hamlyn).

However unusual or outrageous some of Sabine's stories may appear, there is always a strong element of fact running through them and the reader is left to ponder where Sabine really stood on such matters. In serious Folklore circles, some appear to have regarded him merely as an amateur, who catered for the public appetite.

More down to earth matters like the management of the household were in Grace's domain and Sabine left it in her capable hands. Grace was very practical and took firm control of all arrangements, including the supervision of the staff. She did not like waste or unnecessary extravagance and wisely kept the only key to the well-stocked store cupboard tightly secured to a chain around her waist. It was not unknown for Sabine to be extravagant in his ways and this annoyed Grace, who told him so. (How could he complain after informing Grace's parents that he wanted someone who would save him a £100 a year, not one who would spend it!).

The estate and surrounding countryside had a plentiful supply of game so there was never any shortage of pheasant or hare for the dining table. The gardeners also kept the kitchen well supplied with seasonal fruit and vegetables. Although many of the country parsons enjoyed the thrill of the local hunt, Sabine did not partake. However, he allowed members of the hunt on his land, supplied them with refreshment and permitted his children to follow them on any spare horse they could get their hands on.

After loosing Pengelly, Sabine employed Charlie Dunstan in his place. Charlie was a Morris dancer and as he took his master on his rounds he was said to be adept at finding his way into the kitchen for a drop of cider. It was Charlie's job to ensure that suitable transport was always available, be it a horse, dogcart, phaeton or the large family coach. He was also responsible for the stables and these were spring cleaned annually for the children to take part in pantomimes and sketches organised for parents and friends.

For formal occasions Sabine wore a tri-corn hat, fancy stitched jacket, frilly shirt, knee breeches, white silk stockings, black patent buckled shoes and carried a cane. Grace dressed in a long, dark coloured dress trimmed with a, white lace collar secured

69. Baring-Gould being conveyed on his parish rounds by coachman Charlie Dunstan,

with a large, neck brooch and matching accessories. Her best, black hats came from Liberty's of London.

The coachman also wore a uniform comprising a top hat with cockade, long, buttoned overcoat, highly polished black boots and a slender horsewhip. The stagecoach was an impressive sight and, as Sabine and Grace travelled through the villages, the children waved to them.

In Victorian times the rural church was central to people's lives and over the years Sabine increased the size of the small congregation whom he regarded as his family. The seating arrangements at St Peter's Church [one hundred sittings] also followed a strict protocol. The Baring-Gould family and Lavinia occupied the front, centre seats. Behind them came the Sperling family of Coombe Trenchard House, then the doctor and any visitors. The staff of the Baring-Gould household occupied the short seats near the pulpit and the tenant farmers and their families sat beyond them. Local family names regularly associated with the church were: Davy, Dawe, Ball, Truscott, Whitwell, Hamley, Palmer and Wivell.

Cicely Baring-Gould was the organist for many years and her father led the choir with his fine baritone voice. Sabine's curate and Step-brother, Arthur Baring-Gould, regarded Sabine as a most excellent preacher. He also recalled that week after week, he found two little cotton-wool plugs on Sabine's desk and when he asked what they were for Sabine replied.

'Oh, you know that dear Mary Jane, when she is in the choir I simply can't stand it, so I put them in my ears.'

People travelled many miles to listen to Sabine's pithy, eight-minute sermons, each containing one simple point that was driven home. If a visiting preacher failed to make his main point within ten minutes Sabine would pointedly look at his pocket watch and then conclude the sermon on the grounds that it was no good! Such autocratic behaviour must have caused considerable embarrassment to visiting clergy.

After the Sunday service, a parliament met outside the church to exchange messages and gossip. Churchwarden Mr Davy [62] once recalled that Sabine would not organise fund raising events for church projects, much preferring parishioners to give what they could.

At Whitsuntide the celebrations included field sports and Lavinia Baring-Gould put on a traditional bun fight across the fields at Ardoch Lodge. Sabine particularly enjoyed teasing his step-mother and once left a letter in her pew from Lord Kitchener, in the name of the King, requisitioning Ruby, her elderly chestnut horse for the British Army. She was completely taken in by the hoax.

The highlight of the children's day at Whitsuntide was a scramble for handfuls of sweets and money that was thrown across the field. Celebrations came to a close when the children were rounded up and marched home down the lane to Lew House singing *Onward Christian Soldiers*.

It was an age of unabashed snobbery. Curtseys and the touching of the forelock was commonplace and children were expected to know their place. This applied particularly to the Baring-Gould children who, above all, had to be punctual for meals and well behaved at the dining table. In other respects their rural lifestyle gave them a large amount of freedom-to ride horses, climb trees, visit friends and secretly smoke tobacco. Rafting on the quarry lake was a popular activity until one of the choirboys tipped the girls into the deep water and they almost drowned. This prompted Sabine to declare the quarry out of bounds and the message was re-enforced with rumours that huge eels lived there. Reflecting on Sabine's time at Horbury, did the rumour of the Padfoot that supposedly lurked around the Storrs Hill area help drive Grace into Sabine's protective arms as they walked across the fields to the Brig Mission together?

At bedtime the younger children were rounded up and scrubbed pink and clean in a tin bath before the kitchen fire. During supper Grace played nursery rhymes on the piano and then it was off to bed. We have heard that Sabine was strict with his children, in whom he often put the fear of God. He was particularly strict with his sons, who were expected to leave home after completing their education at local grammar schools.

Edward Sabine, who was the eldest son left for the United States where he married and raised a family. However, he returned to England around 1900, where his children were educated and he had business interests in London. Julian worked for the Rajah of Sarawak and in 1903 he led a column of the 2nd Division at Rejang. Despite heavy losses Julian successfully fought off the rebel Dayaks. William Drake became the British Vice-consul in Minneapolis and his son, William S. Baring-Gould, was a writer and a recognised authority on Sherlock Holmes. Henry (Harry) died of fever in Borneo in 1913 aged 28 years.

70. Edward Baring-Gould (1871 - 1957)

The youngest son, John Hilary received a spanking from his father for stealing a washerwoman's tub to sail on the lake at Lew and accompanied his father on geological digs on Dartmoor. John went to Rhodesia in 1952 after spending most of his life as a rubber planter in Malaya. During the First World War he served as a captain in the North Devon Yeomanry and later in the Royal Flying Corps. He shot down four enemy aircraft before being shot down and injured himself by one of Baron Von Richthofen's circus. He got on well with his father who was normally serious and strict, but who also enjoyed playing practical jokes on him.

With the exception of Beatrice, who died in infancy, the remaining nine daughters all married and had children.

71. Dunsland House, Holsworthy, Devon, the former home of Harvey and Mary Dickinson (nee Baring-Gould).

As mentioned earlier, Mary, the eldest daughter was married to Harvey Dickinson and lived at Dunsland House, North Devon, which features in Sabine's book *An Old English Home.* At the time of Mary's marriage, Sabine was distressed to learn that Dunsland House was to be put up for sale after being occupied by the same family for over nine hundred years. Sabine wrote to Harvey advising him against the sale and it was withdrawn. Unfortunately his intervention merely delayed the inevitable, because the house had to be sold after the Second World War to meet death duties.

Dunsland was purchased and restored by the National Trust and Mary's son

72. Vera Baring-Gould born in 1875

Bickford, returned much of the original furniture, paintings and large library. When Bickford became Rector of Lew Trenchard in 1961 he re-published the *Guide to St Peter's Church* and wrote a biography of his grandfather entitled *Sabine Baring-Gould, Squarson, Writer, Folklorist* [63].

The final chapter of Dunsland was written in 1967 when the house and contents, including many of Sabine's first editions, were destroyed by fire. This tragedy prompted Bickford to write the history of his ancestral home but he died in 1975 before it was complete. Twenty years later his nephew published *The Dunsland Saga* [64].

Second daughter, Margaret (Daisy) married Guy Newman who was rector of Lew Trenchard between 1946 and 1961 prior to Bickford Dickinson. Third daughter Beatrice died in infancy and has already received mention.

Fourth daughter, Vera, was a very beautiful and gentle woman who played the harp and the piano and was married to Arthur King by her father at St Peter's Church, Lew Trenchard on 29th October 1902. Arthur was from a long line of physicians at Stratton near Bude, and the wedding was a notable event in the social calendar. They had a daughter, Joan, and Arthur was Master of the Tetcott Hounds for many years. The fifth daughter, Barbara, married Laurie Burnard, the son of Sabine's close friend, Robert Burnard. Again Sabine conducted the wedding ceremony held in the English Church at Dinan, Brittany.

The sixth daughter Diana

73. Barbara Baring-Gould born in 1880.

became Mrs Hugh Maxwell-Batten. They lived in Borneo where her husband worked for the white Rajahs and Sabine wrote of them in the History of Sarawak [65].

Felicitas, the seventh daughter, married Captain Sidney Eyre and when he died married Frank Berkeley-Wily. Joan the eighth daughter became the wife of Bill Priestley, who worked in India. Cicely the ninth daughter, married Colonel Frank Newport Tinley, who also served in India and one of their two daughters was Cicely (Image) Briggs. Grace [junior] was the youngest daughter and inherited rheumatoid arthritis from her mother. Grace was sweet and gentle and married Major Charles Calmady-Hamlyn of Leawood Estate, Bridestowe, Devon.

At times the Baring-Gould household must have seemed overrun by family and suitors!

Although Sabine was very strict with his family, he liked children and took an interest in their development. A typical example of this comes from his granddaughter Joyce Rawstorn (daughter of Joan Baring-Gould) whom he taught a valuable lesson. Joyce recalls:

Diana [her sister] *and I had gone to his room as usual, to say goodnight.*

I asked: 'Please, Grampy, can we do your hair for dinner?' and he agreed.

So, proceeding with many small pieces of pink and blue baby ribbon, which I had specially cut, we tied his hair up in little tufts all over his head. He promised us faithfully that he would go down to dinner and keep it thus all-night. As usual, we walked down the long gallery to the head of the front stairs, where we kissed him goodnight, and said, 'Promise!'

He then went downstairs and into the dining room.

After dinner, the butler announced that two guests were waiting in the drawing room and when Sabine rose to his feet the Butler exclaimed: 'Your hair, Sir!'

Nevertheless, Grampy kept his promise to us – neither excusing nor explaining his appearance – and also as promised, the bows stayed on until breakfast; the lesson being always to keep a promise, come what may, and never pass on a child's secrets, however funny they may be.

Sabine was a strong supporter of the squire system and knew that it worked extremely well so long as the partnership between the squire and his tenants operated fairly, with loyalty going down as well as up! As squire, Sabine was in a position to wield considerable authority over those answerable to him. Add to this his role as spiritual advisor and he was omnipotent. Who would dare oppose such a man or even upset him, knowing he could completely ruin their lives?

How did Sabine exercise this authority? Did he exclude people if their faces didn't fit? Did he ensure compliance with his wishes by subtle pressures? Was he fair and forgiving to those who failed to attend church or if their attendance lapsed without good cause? It is in these areas that Sabine's true nature and character may be assessed.

Those people who knew and worked for him regarded him as a wise and trusted adviser, who was caring and considerate. They welcomed, loved and some even idolised him! He looked after past employees and their dependants and his strong social conscience drew him to those in genuine need. In times of emergency his transport and staff were always available and in one instance he sponsored a deserving youngster for many years on a vocational training course. His standing in the community and strong sense of public duty were also reflected in his appointment as a Justice of the Peace for the County of Devon. Many years after leaving Hurstpierpoint School he also continued to receive the thanks of his ex-pupils.

As a young vicar, Sabine certainly gave the dissenters a hard time in his novels but in later life declared openly in the newspaper that he had always tried to be absolutely fair to dissenters as well as church people; not showing favour to one, more than the other.

Image Briggs describes the relationship of Sabine and Grace through accounts of her mother, Cicely Baring-Gould, who nursed Grace toward the end of her life. Image refers to Grace's unquestionable loyalty to her husband, but also to the heartache she felt by not being really close to all her children, because a nurse was always on hand to take over as soon as they were weaned.

Of Course marital roles have changed greatly since Victorian times and just where Grace's love for her husband became a duty will never be known. It is apparent that Sabine had little awareness of the sensitivities of marriage and Image says that Grace felt this, but never complained. Having said that, there is also a story that Sabine and Grace hadn't been married long when she asked the vicar who married them to *unmarry* them, because she found her husband's temper and incompetence around the house too much to put up with.

When Grace's fifteenth and last child Grace [junior] was born in 1891, her eldest daughters already had children of their own and they were quite surprised when their mother inquired of them how they managed to keep the number of pregnancies down. In her innocence, Grace seems to have simply accepted that children were the natural fruits of marriage and found such matters difficult to discuss.

Mrs Bertha Brown, who was brought up on the Home Farm at Lew Trenchard used to see Grace dressed in a black dress gathering wood in the glen. She remembers her as a charming and friendly little lady, with a warm soft voice that bore no hint of her former Yorkshire accent. Bertha can recall happy times at Lew House when the red carpet was put out for weddings and great balls were held, at which her mother assisted with the cooking. She also recalls teas on the lawns when huge copper kettles and silver teapots were brought out.

Sabine always showed an interest in the children and attended the village school to talk to them in his quiet and gentle voice. He baptised Bertha and married her mother twice. Her father, William Hamley, who managed the Home Farm considered Sabine a good landlord and said he was wonderful to his workers. Similar sentiments have been expressed by many others including Tom Kelloway, who was Sabine's footman, and his wife, Joan, Kelloway, who nursed John and Grace (junior) Baring-Gould.

Although none of Grace's personal letters have been found in the Baring-Gould papers, a series of five letters written to her father and her step-sister Alice around

1900 have recently come to notice through Alice's son, Ivor Atkins.

The letters are newsy and formal in the sense that Grace invariably refers to Sabine as *my husband*. It is also noticeable that in none of them does she make mention of her own activities and feelings.

In one undated Christmas letter [1901 or 2] (see appendix E) Grace informs her father Joseph that they have recently returned home from France [Dinan] where, ... *it is horrid not being able to speak to or understand what people are saying, Grace [her daughter] has got on well with her French. She went to French school in the morning and to an English lady in the afternoon, she could make herself understood very fairly well.*

Grace inquires about her Step-sister Sarah [Larrad] who had been ill and mentions her sister-in-law Blanche [wife of Grace's brother Thomas who lived in Germantown Philadelphia where Thomas was a crane operator in the steel works]. After inquiring about her step-mother, Grace comments: *it is very, very cold weather here, I think it is much colder than in France as it is more damp cold and seems to get right into ones bones, but it changes so rapidly frosty one day and rain the next. I think my husband is really better for the change though he got his cough back a little in France we had a good deal of fog and rain the last two months we were there.*

Grace's lifestyle must have made it difficult for her to relate to the acivities of her her privileged children without stirring feelings of jealousy or resentment in the minds of her own less fortunate relatives and friends.

We have heard that Grace was generous at Christmas and occasionally visited Horbury. For some unknown reason she did not attend her father's funeral in 1904, but two years later she was at the christening of her namesake, Grace Taylor Oakland, who was the daughter of Grace Baring-Gould's step-sister, Emma, of Carlton Street, Horbury. On this occasion, Sabine gave Emma and her two sisters a golden sovereign each. Emma's daughter, Nora Sissons, later wrote: *Grace [Baring-Gould] was a good woman gifted with a deal of plain common sense and the love of a great man must have brought her through great ordeals and the faith and love of our blessed Lord.*

In the years up to the First World War the Baring-Goulds outwardly enjoyed a good lifestyle. However, hardly a year went by without the house and estate being the subject of improvement or repair and, as a consequence of this, Grace was forever cleaning up and dealing with disruptions.

In 1913 Sabine created a rose garden and relocated a sacred well in the stream that runs into the quarry. Such wells were another of Sabine's specialities and he gave advice on the restoration of the fifteenth century well-chapel of St Clether, reputed to be the largest in Cornwall. He must have regarded this project very highly, because in his will he made a provision for it to be maintained.

Sabine described another well at Altarnun as: *One of the most famous of Cornwall's many wells; its waters are deemed specific for madness. The patient is placed with his back to the water, and then violently thrust in and soused with vigour. Prayers are said over him; and it is possible in some cases the shock might cure, but in more cases it will have certainly done injury!* [66].

After Sabine had visited Lourdes he commented, *that in many cases the imagination acting on the nervous system acts curatively goes without saying. It is that which really operates in the faith cures and in the Lourdes miracles* [67].

Sadly, Grace increasingly suffered from the effects of rheumatoid arthritis. Although given the latest sulphur bath treatment, she eventually became bed-bound and Sabine engaged a private nurse to attend her. Sabine is said to have been somewhat detached about Grace's condition, treating her health and welfare as the responsibility of others. This cannot be denied, but Sabine did at least spend some time with Grace, because she dictated letters to him when no longer able to write because of her illness.

The fact that the large house was cold and damp did not help and, although her son Edward arranged for central heating to be installed, it never worked properly. When he offered to have it repaired, his mother could not face the upheaval so nothing more was done.

The commencement of the First World War in 1914 took the young men away from the countryside, hastening many changes to what had formerly been a static and orderly way of life. Some of Sabine's sons and sons-in-law were drafted into the forces and as Sabine followed newspaper reports of hostilities, he was saddened by the destruction of a Europe he knew so well.

By the age of 65 years Grace was so incapacitated by rheumatism that she was totally reliant on others. On 21st December 1915 Sabine wrote to Grace's sister Susan (Douglas): *I am sorry to say that Grace is perfectly helpless. She cannot use her hands and has to be fed like a baby, and lies night and day on her back and cannot move. Her sight and hearing*

74. *Holy Well in the garden of Lew Trenchard House.*

are also failing her somewhat. Happily she has got a good nurse...

When Grace passed away on 8th April 1916 Sabine wrote to Susan; S*he had a peaceful end at the last and died as I, with a broken heart, was reading over her the communicating prayer. She was looking forward to making her Easter Communion, but it was not to be. After 40 years of travelling together on life's journey in great union of heart and soul, I feel utterly as if I had no more to care for in this world.*

Sabine also wrote to Grace's stepsister, Emma Oakland: *We have had a long life's journey together. Married in May 1868 we had 48 years of great union of heart and soul. Till last year it never occurred to me that it was possible that she would be taken before me. She lies now in a double grave and I trust, when God calls me, to be laid by her side.*

Sabine truly adored Grace and her loss had a profound effect upon him. He had her headstone inscribed with the Latin epitaph *Half My Life*. They had complemented each other so well, he often impulsive and irritable and she so modest and unaffected. Unfortunatley none of Sabine's letters to Grace appear to have survived.

A photograph of the Baring-Gould household taken around 1914 poignantly epitomises the transformation of Grace from a charming, unaffected child of the poor into the gracious hostess of Lew Trenchard. The words of Image Briggs describe Grace's unusual situation so aptly: *Her only woman friend was Mrs Sperling of Coombe Trenchard. It was a terrible time of genteel snobbishness. She remained detached as much as possible, yet no one ever forgot her humble beginnings. Even though she could not be faulted in her work as the Lady of the Manor, giving gentle concern to everyone.*

The Times newspaper carried a report of Grace's death and when her personal estate was announced it exceeded two thousand pounds.

If only Sabine could have written the hymn *Amazing Grace.*

75. *Squarson Baring-Gould and wife Grace, (5th & 6th from left front row) with family and staff outside Lew Trenchard House circa 1914.*

Chapter 14

Life Without Grace

It had never been in Sabine's reckoning that Grace would pre-decease him and her loss badly affected him, both psychologically and physically. His literary output practically ceased and as he struggled to run the large household alone, his daughter Cicely took over as housekeeper. It was an arrangement that suited them both because Cicely was about to marry Captain Frank Newport Tinley before he left to take command of the Devonshire Native Cavalry in Flanders.

The war was now affecting everyone. Many items were in short supply or unobtainable and Sabine and his curate also found themselves spending many hours comforting relatives of war casualties.

In November 1918 Sabine received news of the death of his old friend, Gatrill. They had met at the Brig Mission in 1867 and over the years he had deputised for Sabine during family holidays and accompanied him on at least five European jaunts.

When Gatrill left Horbury in 1876 he went to Greenhithe and four years later he took over from Sabine at Mersea. Following further livings at Mistley (1882-8) and Stanway, Essex (1888-1910), he retired to Haywards Heath and produced a book of sermons entitled *Echoes* [68]. Sabine wrote in the preface: *I have known Reverend J. M. Gatrill for a great many years and have appreciated highly his ability as a preacher. He is always thoughtful and impressive and it would be hard to find better types of sermons as patterns by which young preachers should form their style.*

Sabine's friends and contemporaries were now slipping away fast. As the war threatened many of the values he held so dear, he was in danger of becoming isolated and depressed and found it increasingly difficult to process his correspondence. However, he was not one to give in and made a determined effort to correspond regularly with a wide range of people.

Having maintained regular contact with Grace's family, Sabine began to exchange letters with Hannah Taylor, the daughter of Grace's brother, John. She was a young teacher at Eastmoor Junior School, Wakefield and between 1916 and 1922 they exchanged family news, photographs and gifts [69]. Over the next six years Sabine commented on the progress of the war, its effect upon his family, food shortages and the demise of Morris dancing as the young men left for the war.

Sabine also mentioned that he was becoming increasingly forgetful, but this was nothing new to those who knew him. There is a story that during a party at his home he once asked a girl whose pretty child she was and received the tearful reply, *'I'm yours Daddy!'* This gaffe was immortalised in a poem by Charles Causley [70].

1918 was a very good year for Sabine. Hostilities ceased, he received an honorary fellowship from Clare College and his daughter Cicely was safely re-united with her husband, Colonel Tinley. However they soon left for India so that Frank could resume his military career and fortunately their departure coincided with the arrival of Edward and his American wife, Marion.

Perhaps because of his own problems associated with the inheritance of Lew Estate, Sabine had not made any provision for the future of the Estate. Faced with the inevitable question of death duties, it became clear that the property must go to his eldest son Edward and Sabine had his will drawn up accordingly. Unfortunately, Edward was not prepared for this eventuality and had his own business interests in London.

Shortly afterwards, Sabine wrote a pathetic communication to his trusted friend and church organist, Gladys Dawe, drawing attention to his poor health and stating that he was tottering on the edge of the grave [71]. However, the following year he was in much better form and informed Hannah Taylor that, although he was very unsteady on his feet after a fall, he was attending church and inquired whether Horbury Brig church was still flourishing. In April 1922 Sabine took Hannah in his motorcar to visit Mary at Dunsland House. It appears to have been their final meeting.

Sabine celebrated his ninetieth year on 28th January 1923 and, although confined to bed, he greeted his large family and friends. The press were also invited and they kindly depicted him as Devon's Grand Old Man [72].

When everyone was assembled, Sabine explained that twelve of his children were still living and that his nine daughters were all married. Of his three surviving sons, he explained that Edward had served the country from the first day of the war until the last and had been fortunate enough not to be wounded.

Sabine announced the completion of his *Early Reminiscences* (1834-1864) and that another edition covering his middle age was underway. This was published in 1925 after his death, entitled *Further Reminiscences* (1864-1894). He also referred to a recent amalgamation of the parishes of Lew Trenchard and Thrustleton, and that he was busy making the acquaintance of his new parishioners.

Sabine had received birthday messages from children who had visited him that morning and from the Dean and Chapter, the Archdeacon, and the Proctor of Convocation of the Diocese of Exeter. The Devon Association [73] also wrote:

Dear Mr Baring-Gould,

The good wishes of every member of the Devon Association attend your birthday.

76. The Reverend S. Baring-Gould, circa 1914.

We may not claim that the advancement of Science, Literature and Art is an object wide enough to include the whole scope of your work, but we are proud that you have associated yourself with our efforts to fulfil the interest of our corporate being. For your help and example in the past you claim our gratitude and the present volume of Transactions will bear witness that you have not claimed the privilege of advancing years to fail in assistance to fellow-workers.

If there is any formality in this expression of our respect, the fault is in my own choice of words, and not in my own sincere intent nor in the feeling of our Association.

Personally I would beg you to accept my sincerest good wishes and respect.
I am, yours sincerely R. H. Worth.
Hon. Gen. Sec., Devon Association.

Sabine replied:
Many thanks to you and the Association for kind congratulations. Excuse card as for nigh on 3 weeks I have been bed-ridden, and although I hope to be about some day this week, I can now only get up and remain up for about 8 or 10 minutes to write acknowledgements of kind wishes.

Oh! Dartmoor! I have not set foot on it for 4 years. I look at it with yearning eyes from Lew Down, whenever I am there.
Yours truly S. Baring-Gould.

Despite deteriorating health, Sabine finalised work on *Further Reminiscences* and also sent three hymns for publication. One of them was a Christmas carol entitled *Hasten to Bethlehem* and this appeared in the newspapers just before Christmas 1923 [74]. By Christmas morning Sabine was seriously ill. Family and friends assembled outside his bedroom to sing *Hasten to Bethlehem* and this cheered him.

During the early hours of 2nd January 1924 Sabine died. The funeral service was held on the following Saturday and the cortege stretched all the way from Lew House to St Peter's Church where he had served for forty-three years. The service was conducted jointly by his step-brother Arthur, who said prayers and G.H. Arundell (Sabine's curate) who read the lesson. Several of Sabine's hymns were played during the service and the Bishops of Exeter and Plymouth performed the last rites as Sabine was laid to rest beside his beloved Grace.

The inscription on Grace's headstone reads:
"Dimidium Animae Meae"
(Half My Life)

For his headstone Sabine chose:
"Paravi Lucernam Christo Meo"
(I have prepared a lantern for my Christ).

77. The adjoining graves of Sabine and Grace Baring-Gould at St Peter's Church,
Lew Trenchard.

Although it had been sixty years since Sabine left Horbury with his young bride, he was still remembered there with affection. The vicar of St John's Church, at Horbury Brig was George W Brodribb and he opened an appeal to build a new rood screen in Sabine's honour. Contributions were received from the Common Lands Trust and local businesses, but the bulk of the appeal came in small amounts from individuals: two and sixpence in memory of Mehalah, ten shillings from an admirer of Reverend S. Baring-Gould, twelve shillings and sixpence from some mill girls and two guineas from an old schoolboy [75].

While the appeal was ongoing the vicar received a copy of Sabine's *Further Reminiscences*. He commented that the content was disappointing so far as Sabine's time in Horbury was concerned and was not aware that Sabine had actually written an account of his time there, but it had either been excluded from that edition or was intended for a third volume to be published ten years after his death.

When the third volume of Sabine's reminiscences failed to appear in 1934, the press printed the following statement prepared by Sabine's son, Edward:

My father instructed me to revise them carefully and not hesitate to cut parts out or destroy them altogether if, in my opinion it was desirable, and their publication might cause pain to any people mentioned in the volume.

Naturally after his death a diligent search was made for the manuscript but in vain. Inquiry of the maid attending his [Sabine's] room revealed the fact that one morning there was a great quantity of ash in the grate as if a large amount of manuscript had been burned [76].

The missing chapter of Sabine's marriage to Grace must have been controversial for it to be excluded. In its absence, the only known reference to that period of Sabine's life is that contained in the autobiographical novel *Through Flood and Flame* which he wrote while living alone at Dalton.

78. Memorial rood screen to Sabine Baring-Gould at St John's Church, Horbury Bridge.

On 1st May 1926 Sabine's memorial was installed by Bishop Frodsham of Halifax [77] who had known Sabine personally:

The first thing was his undoubted keenness, - he was a really hard worker. In 1866 they had not that beautiful little church, and the mission room at Horbury Bridge was only a house, services being held in the upper room. Folk said that not only was the upper room crowded when Mr Baring-Gould was preaching, but the, congregation sat on the stairs and some outside in the street, trying to listen.

One elderly man, who was only a small boy in 1866, remembered those services and was struck by the fact that everybody was so quiet that they could have heard a pin drop. That man also remembered the curious smile with which Mr Baring-Gould used to look at them as he saw them listening to him. Yes, for all his stern features he had a very winning smile, which drew people's hearts to him like a magnet. The deepest and strongest appeal being made to the spirituality which lay deep and strong in the Northern character - it might be hidden for a while, but sooner or later it showed itself.

The Bishop referred to Sabine: *As a voluminous and bold writer, whose humour was sometimes bizarre and irony relentless. They were proud to remember Onward Christian Soldiers written for the children of Horbury Bridge - the little children who found the way long and steep to their Whitsuntide school feast, and who found, as Baring-Gould knew they would, that the way would be shortened by a song. How many who sang the hymn, considered how the simple directness of the words revealed the strong heart of the writer*

Bishop Frodsham forecast that: *The hymn would probably be sung as long as English Christianity lived and might easily remain as a possession of our race when Baring-Gould has been forgotten.*

A year later, Oscar Berry who had taken part in the first Whitsuntide procession as a young boy, presented St John's Church with memorabilia connected with Sabine's processional hymn. These items, along with the wooden processional cross and the memorial rood screen, may be seen by arrangement with the vicar at St Peter's Church, Horbury. (For further information see appendix F)

Chapter 15

Baring-Gould - The Man

An itinerant education and European travel gave Sabine a cosmopolitan outlook and a curiosity for diverse subjects that he shared with others through his vocation, lectures and particularly his writing, which appears to have flowed without effort.

Having followed his calling into the Church of England, Sabine successfully opened the Brig Mission leaving the legacy of a famous hymn. Selecting his future bride from a humble background, Sabine invested in the future by sending her to be trained in the ways of the middle classes. Grace responded positively and they went on to enjoy a long and happy marriage, blessed with many fine children.

After receiving his inheritance in 1872 and moving to Lew Trenchard in 1881, Sabine devoted the next forty-three years of his life to improving the fabric of his estate and the spirituality of his parishioners. Rarely constrained by domestic issues, he was able to balance his clerical role against his wide range of interests.

Several generations of readers grew up with Sabine's books and those who accused him of churning out pot-boiler novels were right – he converted the rewards into bricks and mortar. Those who said he had a magpie mind - jumping from one obscure subject to another were also right. It was his fresh observation and versatility that appealed to readers. Yes, there were better contemporary novelists and he may have been somewhat cavalier when writing *The Vicar of Morwenstowe*, but few were able to match his output or range.

Sabine possessed great charm, was loved and respected by those who knew him and had a good sense of humour with a leaning toward irony. Some say he was also a great romancer, but this was often so skilfully blended with fact that it was almost impossible to define the boundaries.

He was also a complex, controlled and eccentric man with a deep understanding of people and character. Sabine rarely engaged in small talk and as a writer rarely stepped outside the role of commentator. Even his weighty volumes of *Reminiscences* give little insight into the inner man and, although the missing section of them may have addressed this matter, this is merely conjecture.

Behind Sabine's façade of intriguing stories, interesting facts and unusual activities lay an inner core which scores of comprehensive media interviews never penetrated. Even his talented and informed stepbrother, Arthur Baring-Gould [78], admitted defeat when he attempted to write a biography of him, commenting; *How difficult it is for me or indeed anyone to write any sort of life of Sabine.* He was right! Apart from his parents, Grace, loyal friend, Gatrill, and perhaps Daniel Radford and Robert Burnard, few people ever came close to really knowing the real Sabine Baring-Gould.

After sixty years of ministry the church never saw fit to offer Sabine preferment and those who made such decisions may well have felt there was no shortage of reasons for this. However, personal accounts from the parish indicate that Sabine was a good minister and a wise and trusted counsellor and three successive Church of England biographers have not found cause to challenge this [79].

After Sabine's death the Western Morning News of 5th January 1924 wrote of ministry:

It is no exaggeration to say that the Diocese of Exeter has lost its best known and most distinguished priest, and the Church of England its most gifted author. Other clergy have been more learned in special departments of theology and historic knowledge but none have been able to write with such widespread knowledge of all branches of literature. He was not a 'broad minded' man who tried to get on well with everybody, for he had most definite religious convictions, and was unsparing in his criticism of those with whom he differed. His courage, candour, and outspokenness gained for him the admiration of all. May God grant him eternal rest and peace.

While Sabine had been busy ministering to others, travelling abroad, studying, or writing it must not be overlooked that Grace was always there to support him and run the home. Although undoubtedly spending many hours alone, Grace appears to have accepted this and, who knows, with such a large family to mother she may have occasionally welcomed the solitude! Churchwarden Davy [80] said of Grace: she *was a lovely woman if ever there was one. Even in her later days there was a beauty about her which you had to admire. It came from deep within.*

Perhaps it was these very qualities that Sabine had discovered when they first met. It has been said that Sabine never knowingly overshadowed Grace, who during their forty-eight years of marriage was the perfect foil for him. He was often impulsive and strict and she so calm, natural and loving. Although Sabine may have appeared hard on his wife and family by dashing off for long periods alone, it was in his nature and there were undoubtedly compensations. Sabine and Grace were clearly very happy together. Who could ask for more?

Baring-Gould's extraordinary life had been influenced by many factors: his, parentage, learning, travel, teaching, marriage, religion and living and working in different regions of England. There is no denying that he loved his native Devon and rightly so. He also made his mark in Essex where he was inspired to write his best selling novel, Mehalah. During a relatively short time in Yorkshire he was ordained, opened a mission, wrote hymns and found a wife, all of which made a deep and lasting impression upon him. He, in turn, left an indelible mark in the Yorkshire psyche.

Sabine Baring-Gould lived his ninety years to the full, providing for his wife and family, undertaking his ministry and entertaining his readers. Whether seen as a husband, father, squarson, writer, traveller, hymn writer, collector of songs, antiquarian or amateur archaeologist he was a good and truly remarkable man.

Had Sabine channelled all his boundless energy into one area of activity he could have virtually achieved anything!

Chapter 16

Epilogue

The gross value of Sabine's estate amounted to just over £16,000 and his eldest son Edward was the main beneficiary. Sabine also left two bequests: £50 for the up-keep of the well-chapel at St Clether Parish Church, Cornwall and the donation of his books on the Celtic Saints to the Bishop Phillpot's Library in Truro [81].

While his son, Edward and Edward's wife, Marion were at Lew House they carried out many improvements and even consulted Miss Gertrude Jekyll, [82] the famous horticulturalist, for advice on the garden. Unfortunately when Marion died in 1931 things were never the same. Their three children, Sabine Linton, Edward (Ted) and Adele all went to live in America and Edward moved up to London to concentrate on his business interests.

Edward subsequently was re-married to Maud Caroline Underhay and Lew Trenchard estate was left in the hands of trustees and agents. Following a succession of tenants the house had become so neglected by the end of the Second World War that it was almost uninhabitable. Valuable household items had been damaged or taken away and when it was discovered that water had leaked into the library, many personal papers and books were removed and burned.

During the 1950s Reginald and Elsie Paynter and their friend Jim Purdy fell in love with the house and took over the lease. After many hours labour and much expense they gradually recovered the situation and in the mid 60s opened a restaurant. They enjoyed a moderate degree of success, providing cream teas and catering for wedding parties but received little reward.

In 1975 the lease was taken over by Sabine's granddaughter, Image Briggs, who, along with her husband, daughter Sallie and friends, fought long

79. Cicely (Image) Briggs

and hard to bring the premises up to the standard of a first class hotel. Unfortunately, they encountered a series of totally unforeseen disasters and despite their best efforts, success eluded them and they closed the hotel in 1980. During the next eight years two more families took over before the arrival of the present occupants in 1988.

Through the efforts of James and Sue Murray Lew House has now been transformed into a first class luxury hotel. It is known as Lewtrenchard Manor and truly reflects the full glory of Sabine's ideal.

When Edward Baring-Gould died in 1957 his son Sabine Linton became 'Tenant for Life'. Following his death in 1972 Lew Trenchard passed to his daughter, Dr Merriol Baring-Gould Almond, who is the present owner.

Through the energy of Mrs Almond and the creation of the Baring-Gould Corporation, Lew Trenchard Estate is now in good hands and its future is in the ascendancy.

80. Dr Merriol Baring-Gould Almond.

The Baring-Gould Family Tree

The forebears & descendants of the BARINGS and the GOULDS of LEW TRENCHARD (abridged)   Appendix A

John GOLD Palestine Crusader circa 1217

Twelve Generations in Male Line

Edward GOULD (1626 - 1667) = Elizabeth (SEARLE) (- 1727)

Sarah GOULD (- 1728/9)

Henry GOULD (1657 - 1735) = Elizabeth (LEGATT) (- 1748) Susannah GOULD (- 1729) = P. TRUSCOTT (- 1758)
"White Lady Ghost"

William GOULD (1679 - 1753) = Elizabeth (DRAKE) (- 1729)

William Drake GOULD (1719 - 1766) = Margaret (BELFIELD) (1711 - 1795) "Old Madam Ghost"

Edward GOULD (1740 - 1788) "The Scamp"   Margaret GOULD (1743 - 1803) = Charles BARING (1742 - 1829)

William B-G   (1805 - 39)
Rev. Charles B-G   (1807 - 81)
Emily Sabine B-G   (18 -2 - 93)
Rev. Alexander B-G   (1814 - 99)

William BARING-GOULD (1770 - 1846) 'Devonshire Adonis'   Diana Amelia (SABINE) (1775 - 1868)
(Took the name BARING-GOULD in 1795)

Margaret B-G (1803 - 1853)   Edward BARING-GOULD 'Silver Poplar' = (1) Sophia Charlotte BOND (1808 - 1863)   = (2) Lavinia (SNOW) (1829 - 1921)
(1804 -1872)

Harriet B-G (1801 - 1857)

Edward Drake BARING-GOULD (1851 - 1887)   Rev. Arthur BARING-GOULD (1866 - 1955)   Leila BARING-GOULD (   )

Margaret Ellen BARING-GOULD (1835 - 1903) = Rev. T.H. MARSH (1843 - 1905)

William (Willy) BARING-GOULD (1836 - 1880)

Sabine BARING-GOULD (1834 - 1924) = Grace Berry TAYLOR (1850 - 1916)

Mary (1869 - 1945)   Margaret (Daisy) (1870 - 1938)   Edward Sabine BARING-GOULD (1871 - 1957) = (1) Marion Darragh (LINTON) (- 1931)
= (2) Maud Caroline (UNDERHAY)(- 1926)

Twelve other siblings as below

Beatrice   (1874 - 1876)
Veronica   (1875 - 1958)
Julian   (1877 - 1929)
William Drake   (1878 - 1922)
Barbara   (-880 -   )
Diana Amelia   (-881 -   )
Felicitas Ayre   (1883 - 1951)
Henry (Harry)   (1885 - 1913)
Joan   (1887 - 1967)
Cicely   (1889 -   )
John Hilary   (1890 -   )
Grace Adele   (1891 - 1948)

Sabine Linton BARING-GOULD (1902 - 1972) = (1) Constance (THRALL)
= (2) Mary Elizabeth (SEARS)

Merriol BARING-GOULD = Douglas ALMOND   Constance Roberta B-G

Catherine Collier (1967 -   )   Elizabeth Merrial (1969 -   )   Douglas Vincent (1970 -   )   Christopher Sabine (1971 -   )

Joseph TAYLOR & Family

First Marriage

Joseph TAYLOR		=	**Hannah TAYLOR**
(1823 - 1904)			(1822 - 1867)

John	(1848 - 1928)	=	Ellen _____
Grace Berry	(1850 - 1916)	=	Sabine BARING-GOULD
Susan	(1852 - 1927)	=	Thomas DOUGLAS
William	(1853 -)	=	Miss HORNSEY
Thomas	(1855 -)	=	Blanche _____
Annie	(1858 -)	=	_____
Benjamin	(1860 - 1861)		
Mary Ann	(1862 -)	=	(1) Robert SMITH
		=	(2) ____ CROSSLAND
Sarah	(1864 -)	=	Albert LARRAD

Second Marriage

Joseph TAYLOR		=	**Bessie BERRY**
(1823 - 1904)			(1832 -)

Elizabeth	(1871 -)	=	_____
Emma	(1873 - 1946)	=	George OAKLAND
Ellen	(1874 - 1874)		
Alice	(1876 -)	=	Alfred BOULBY

Letter dated 16 March 1864 from S Baring Gould to Nathaniel Woodard and reply. By kind permission Lancing College.

1st Sunday after Epiphany

Woodard
*Submit to G.
further.*

Dear Mr Woodard,

Will you kindly give me your advice in the present case — my parents wish to refer the matter of my taking Holy Orders to the arbitration of the Bishop of Exeter, and I hardly know whether to consent, having so decidedly made up my mind to take Orders, & now to have the possibility of unsettling all again.

My father puts the case distinctly to me if I enter the ministry, he tears up his will and leaves the property away from me. That does not trouble me much and I would readily consent to his doing so, if that were all. But he says further, that he feels his loneliness without one of his children near him and his spirits are subject to great depression, as he gets older. My youngest brother leaves him to go to school and he has no companion in his solitude. This is the only difficulty I feel. at the same time the whole desire of my heart

is to take Holy Orders and work at Hurst. Will you tell me your opinion, whether I should allow the case to be submitted to the Bishop & follow his decision as final.

I remain, dear sir,

yours very truly

S. Baring Gould

The Collected Letters & Diaries of George Robert Gissing.

Letter dated 15 April 1888 – to Katie Gissing (Sister-in-law). *'Here is a cutting of some interest. I had no [idea] that Baring-Gould was a man of ancestral estates. Really, his versatility is remarkable; amateur architect to boot! Must be 60 at the very least, I should think.'*

Diary entry 19th April 1888 - ...'and running through(it is not worth reading) Baring-Gould's Red Spider...'

Letter dated 22nd January 1892 - to brother Algernon Gissing.... *'I have tried to read The Gaverocks by Baring-Gould. A worthless production: one is astonished that good type & paper can be wasted on such drivel.'*

Diary Entry 27th May 1892 - ...Reading Baring-Goulds Richard Cable - Poor stuff.

Letter dated 3rd December 1894 - to Algernon ...'Tremendous indictment of Baring-Gould in this week's AthenÆum.' (25 March 1876 pp.417-9). Gissing refers to the review of the Deserts of Southern France in the issue of December 1 (1894): "Of Mr Baring-Gould's volumes [2] there is little to be said, except that they contain a vast amount of ill-arranged information and constitute a rather flagrant example of bookmaking".

Letters: From The Collected Letters of George Gissing. Volumes 3 & 5 Edited by Paul Mattheisen, Arthur C. Young & Pierre Coustillas. Ohio University Press 1992 & 1995.

Diary Entries: From London and the Life of Literature in Late Victorian England. The Diary of George Gissing, Novelist. Edited by Pierre Coustillas, Harvester Press 1978.

By kind permission of Professor Pierre Coustillas.

Sample of Grace Baring-Gould's letters. By kind permission of Ivor Atkins

continued overleaf

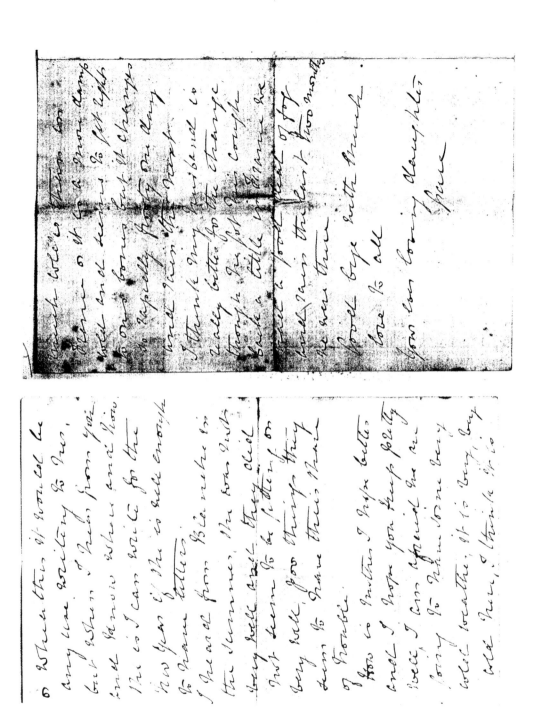

Further information about Baring-Gould

A resurgence of interest in the life of Baring-Gould has resulted in research into his activities, modern reprints of his books, plays based on his novels and events featuring his folkmusic. Further information about these and other activities is available from the following sources:

Lewtrenchard Manor, Lewdown, Nr, Okehampton, Devon EX20 4PN.
www.lewtrenchard.co.uk

Praxis Books. Crossways Cottage, Walterstone, Herefordshire HR2 ODX.
www.rebeccatope.com

Red Spider Music & Dance Group of West Devon. www.redspidercompany.co.uk

Sabine Baring-Gould Appreciation Society (SBGAS). www.sbgas.fsnet.co.uk

SBGAS Hon. Secretary:
Dr Roger Bristow, Davidsland, Brendon Hill, Copplestone, Devon, EX17 5NX.
E-mail Address rbristow@rbristow89.freeserve.co.uk.

SBGAS. Research Co-ordinator:
Keith Lister. E-mail address keith@listerk.freeserve.co.uk

Sabine Baring-Gould Website.
www.greenjack.btinternet.co.uk

St. Peter's Vicarage, Northgate, Horbury, Wakefield, WF4 6AS
www.wakefield.anglican.org

Wren Trust. 1,St James Street, Okehampton, Devon. EX20 1DW. (Music, workshops, song writing and live performances). www.wrentrust.co.uk

Notes and References

1. Pronounced Saybin Baring-Goold. In later life Sabine often omitted the hyphen from his surname.
2. The Mystery of Suffering. Six Lectures by S Baring-Gould. Skeffington & Co.
3. Early Reminiscences p.256 by S. Baring-Gould. Skeffington & Co. 1877.
4. The Oxford Movement founded 1833 (not to be confused with Oxford Group). Led by Oxford high churchmen E.B. Pusey, J. Keble, and J.H. Newman. They issued religious tracts and worked to secure recognition of catholic liturgy and doctrine in the Anglican Church without accepting the authority of the Pope.
5. John Ruskin (1819-1900).
6. Through the Night of Doubt and Sorrow translated by S Baring-Gould from hymn by B.S. Ingeman (1789-1862) Copenhagen Psalmbog 1859.
7. London Illustrated News 24 August 1872.
8. Hurst Johnian 1858-60. By kind permission of Hurstpierpoint School, Sussex.
9. Iceland, Its Scenes and Sagas. Smith, Elder & Co. London. 1863. By kind permission of the Dean and Chapter of York.
10. The Book of Were-Wolves: Being an Account of a Terrible Superstition by S Baring-Gould. Smith Elder & Co. London.
11. Inventing Ruritania. The Imperialism of the Imagination. Vesna Goldsworthy. Yale University Press 1988.
12. Grettir the Outlaw: a story of Iceland. Baring-Gould. Blackie & Son 1890.
13. The reverend Dr. J.B. Dykes 1823-1876.
14. John Carr (1732-1807) architect of York. Carr was born in Horbury, owned quarries there and is buried in the crypt at St Peter's Church.
15. R.L. Arundale papers. W. Yorks. Archive Service, Wakefield Ref. C1039.
16. Wakefield Express 2 February 1867.
17. Area re-named Sitlington in 1929. Includes villages of Netherton, Midgley, Middlestown & Overton.
18. The Additional Curates Society was established in 1837 to fund the employment of curates in poor and populous parishes.
19. Church Times 2 July 1864, p210, p227, 30 July 1864 p243 by kind permission of the Dean and Chapter of York.
20. The Sign July 1920 by kind permission of Courtesy of Chansistor Publications Ltd & WYAS Ref WDP135.
21. Hurst Johnian May 1865 by kind permission of Hurstpierpoint School, Sussex.
22. Further Reminiscences p8. S Baring-Gould The Bodley Head 1925.
23. In the days before churches had crockery people provided their own.
24. Sabine Baring-Gould Appreciation Society(SBGAS). Founded by Reverend David Shacklock in 1989 to enable those interested in Baring-Gould and his work, to share their enthusiasm and spread the interest among others.

25. Abraham Archer, Ford Mill was declared bankrupt in March 1865.

26. A large fire occurred at Poppleton's Mill in August 1865.

27. Life and Letters of J.B. Dykes by J.T.Fowler. John Murray 2nd ed 1897

28. The Small World of Fred Hoyle. Michael Joseph 1986.

29. St Peter's Parish Magazine April 1918.

30. The Yorkshire Post Newspaper, Barker's Yorkshire 22nd March 1997.

31. Now the Day is Over by S. Baring-Gould from a German tune.

32. Through the Night of Doubt and Sorrow translated by S. Baring-Gould from hymn by B.S. Ingeman (1789-1862) Copenhagen Psalmbog 1859.

33. On the Resurrection Morning by S. B-Gould. Tunes by Mansfield & Hornsey.

34. Sleep My Saviour Sleep by S. Baring-Gould. From a Bohemian folk melody.

35. Four lesser known hymns reference W.E. Purcell

36. Hasten to Bethlehem by S. Baring-Gould. A Basque Noel Carol. The Chronicle Newspaper December 15th 1923.

37. Ossett Observer 23rd March 1946. [The Dame School was in Crowther's Buildings (re-named Fernandez Place) off Bridge Road, Horbury].

38. Westminster Gazette 3.1.1924.

39. Munby Man of Two Worlds: The life & Diaries of Arthur F. Munby 1828-1910 by Derek Hudson. Published by J. Murray 1972.

40. The Ossett Observer 15th April 1916.

41. Wakefield Express 29th December 1866.

42. The Battle of Brunanburgh, Yorkshire Archaeological Journal 1913 Vol.22.

43. When the original patterns for these fine windows were auctioned at Christies in February 1992 they raised almost £10,000 each. Christies 20th Century Decorative Arts Department.

44. Further Reminiscences p.16 by S. Baring-Gould. The Bodley Head 1925.

45. The 1865 Wakefield Industrial and Fine Arts Exhibition attended by almost 200,000 people. It led to the establishment of the School of Art and then Wakefield Technical College.

46. Bligh Bond (1861-1945) Sabine's cousin. Mss in possession of New York Public Library Ref 51M139. & Bristol Central Library

47. 1. The Ferns and Fern Allies of Wakefield and its Neighbourhood. By T.W.Gissing. R.Micklethwaite. Wakefield 1862. 2. Materials for a Flora of Wakefield and its neighbourhood. T.W. Gissing. J.V.Voorst. London. 1867.

48. George Gissing English novelist (1857-1903).

49. Pilmoor is now designated as being a Site of Special Scientific Interest.

50. Collected Letters of George Gissing Vols. 3 & 5. Edited by Paul Mattheisen, Arthur C. Young & Pierre Coustillas. Ohio University Press 1992 & 1995.

51. Discovering Exeter 2/St Leonard's by Gilbert Venn. Pp 10 & 13. Exeter Civic Society 1982.

52. Our Friend the Charlatan 1901 Chapman & Hall & The Gissing Newsletter Vol.XXlll, Number 4 October 1987. Article by Anthony Petyt pp 19-24.

53. Further Reminiscences p.139-41. S Baring-Gould The Bodley Head 1925.
54. Wives of Famous Men, The Sunday Companion – undated.
55. Oxford Magazine 18 May 1944 with obituary by F.J.W.
56. Book of notes sent to Professor F.J. Child by Baring-Gould in 1890. Houghton Library, Harvard University. Ref FMS 863.
57. The Daily Graphic 6th February 1892.
58. A Page of Confessions – un-attributed.
59. The Mana of Lew. Cicely Briggs. Praxis Books 1993.
60. Essenes, Samerians, Kahunnas, Egyptians & Quabella.
61. A Book of Ghosts by S Baring-Gould. Methuen & Co London 1904.
62. The Times 25th May 1951.
63. The Parish Church St. Peter, Lew Trenchard & The Rev Sabine Baring-Gould by HC Dickinson.
64. The Dunsland Saga by Bickford HC Dickinson (S.H. Dickinson) James S Porterfield, Barnstaple 1996.
65. The History of Sarawak under its Two White Rajah's 1839-1908 H. Sotheran & Co. London. 1909.
66. Cornwall by Arthur L. Salmon. Methuen London 1927.
67. Devonshire Characters & Strange Events S Baring-Gould M.A. The Bodley Head 1908.
68. Echoes. 24 Plain sermons by J.M.Gatrill. Skeffington. London 1912.
69. Bodleian Library. Ms.Eng.lett.d.298 – June 1983.
70. The Reverend Sabine Baring-Gould by Charles Causley.
71. Article by Wesley Colwill in SBGAS Newsletter 9.
72. Western Morning News & Mercury dated January 1923 in article entitled Rev S Baring-Gould Quiet Celebration of 89th Birthday.
73. Transactions of the Devon Association Obituary Notices 1924.
74. Daily Chronicle & Daily Telegraph 15 December 1923.
75. St. Peter's Parish Magazine August 1924. WYAS Ref WDP135.
76. Evening Echo 5th February 1934.
77. Ossett Observer 8th May 1926.
78. Mss dated 1948 by Rev Arthur Baring-Gould by kind permission of the late Cedric Baring-Gould.
79. 1. Onward Christian Soldier. A life of Baring-Gould by W E Purcell. Longmans Green & Co. London. 1957.
    2. Sabine Baring-Gould. Squarson, Writer & Folklorist. Bickford H. C. Dickinson. David & Charles. Newton Abbot. 1970.
    3. Now The Day Is Over The Life and Times of Sabine Baring-Gould. Harold Kirk-Smith. Richard Kay. Lincolnshire. 1997.
80. The Times 25th May 1951.
81. Details of Celtic Saints, Irish, Welsh, Cornish, Breton & Scottish.
82. Gertrude Jekyll 1843-1932.

Bibliography

A Devon Family The Story of the Aclands. Anne Acland. Phillimore. London 1981.

Archaeol Cambrensis 5th Series, Vol. 17, 1900.

Baring-Gould Family Papers.

Belfry. Sunday Magazine Vol. 24.

Best of Essex Countryside E.V. Scott. County Guide Publications. Letchworth 1976.

Bibliography of the Works of Sabine Baring-Gould by C. R. Bristow.

Book of Brittany by S Baring-Gould Methuen & Co. London 1901.

Book of Dartmoor by S Baring-Gould. Methuen & Co. London 1900.

Book of Ghosts by S. Baring-Gould. Methuen & Co. London 1904.

Book of North Wales by S Baring-Gould Methuen & Co London 1903.

Book of the Rhine from Cleve to Mainz by S. Baring-Gould. Methuen & Co. London 1906.

Book of Were-Wolves: being an Account of a Terrible Superstition. Smith Elder & Co. London 1865.

British Folklorists. A History by R.M. Denson.

Building of a Church Holy Trinity Nice 1870-1970. G.K.Wilkinson 1970.

Camp Hancock Edition of Trench Camp, 101st. United States Cavalry Headquarters.

Celtic Saints, Journal of the Royal Institution of Cornwall vol. 14 1899 & The Celtic Monasteries.

Chamber's Journal 19th May 1894.

Cheap Jack Zita a story of Ely Fens by S. Baring-Gould. Methuen & Co. London 1893.

Church of S Peter & S. Leonard Horbury Anniversary Brochure 1944.

Church Revival. Thoughts Thereon & Reminiscences. By S. Baring-Gould. Methuen. London 1914.

Cliff Castles and Cave Dwellings of Europe by S. Baring-Gould. Seeley & Co. London 1911.

Collected Letters of George Gissing Vol. 3 1886-88 April 15 1888. Edited by Paul F. Matheisen, Arthur C. Young & Pierre Coustillas. Ohio University Press 1992.

Complete Peerage. Gibbs 1916.

Cornwall by Arthur L. Salmon. Methuen. London 1927.

Coronation Souvenir by the Rev. S. Baring-Gould. Skeffington & Son. London 1911.

Country Life – 31st March 1966.

County Folklore collected & edited by Mrs Gutch. D.Nutt 1901.

Deserts of Southern France by S. Baring-Gould. Methuen. London 1894.

Devon Family The Story of the Aclands by Anne Acland. Phillimore & Co. 1981.

Devonshire Characters & Strange Events by Sabine Baring-Gould. J. Lane. London 1908.

Discovering Exeter 5/Sidwell Street by Hazel Harvey. Exeter Civic Society 1986.

Discovering Exeter 2/St Leonard's by Gilbert Venn. Exeter Civic Society 1982.

Dunsland Saga by Bickford H.C. Dickinson by S. H. Dickinson. James S. Porterfield, Barnstable 1996.

Early Reminiscences by S. Baring-Gould. J. Lane. London 1924.

Encyclopedia of Dates & Events Pascoe. Lee & Jenkins E.U.P 1968.

English Folk-Songs for Schools collected and arranged by S. Baring-Gould & Cecil J. Sharp. J. Curwen. London 1906.

English Minstrelsie T.C.& G.C Jack Edinburgh. 8 Vols. 1895-7.

Ferns and Fern Allies of Wakefield and its Neighbourhood. By T.W.Gissing. R.Micklethwaite. Wakefield 1862.

Further Reminiscences (1864-1894) by S Baring-Gould. J. Lane. London 1925.

Garland of Country Song by S. Baring-Gould & H. Fleetwood Sheppard. Methuen & Co. London 1895.

Germany The Story of The Nations Series by T.Fisher. Unwin. London 1886.

Gissing Newsletter October 1987. Vol XX111 No.4 by Anthony Petyt.

Gladstone Diaries 1825-96 by M.D. Foot & H. Mathew. OUP 1978.

Gould Methuen & Co. London 1906.

Graphic February 6 1892 - In the Land of Teck.

Grettir the Outlaw: a story of Iceland. S. Baring-Gould. Blackie & Son. London 1890.

History of Sarawak under its Two White Rajahs 1839-1908 by S Baring-Gould with CA Bampfylde. Sotheran & Co. London 1909.

Hurst Johnian 1858-60.

Hurstpierpoint College 1849-1995. Peter King. Phillimore. 1997.

Iceland, It's Scenes and Sagas. S. Baring-Gould. Smith Elder & Co. London 1863.

In the Roar of the Sea: a Tale of the Cornish Coast by S. Baring-Gould. Methuen & Co. London 1892.

Inventing Ruritania. The Imperialism of the Imagination by Vesna Goldsworthy. Yale University Press 1988.

John Ruskin An Illustrated Life 1819-1900. James S Dearden.

Letter in possession of Vicar of St. Peter's Church, Horbury published in Parish Magazine April 1918.

Lew Trenchard, The Manor House, The Church and Baring-Gould published privately by S. Gordon Monk Plymouth 1961.

Life and Letters of J.B. Dykes by J.T.Fowler. John Murray 1897.

Lives of the Saints by S Baring-Gould. 15 volume edition 1872-7.John Hodges. London.

Illustrated London News June 15th 1850.

Mana of Lew by Cicely Briggs. Praxis Books 1993.

Materials for a Flora of Wakefield and its neighbourhood by T.W. Gissing. J.V.Voorst. London. 1867.

Mehalah a Story of the Salt Marshes by S. Baring-Gould. Smith Elder, London 1880.

Miscellaneous letters of S. Baring-Gould dated February 1899-1904. By kind permission of Ivor Atkins.

Munby Man of Two Worlds; The Life & Diaries of Arthur F Munby 1828-1910 by Derek Hudson. J. Murray 1972.

Mystery of Suffering Six lectures by S. Baring-Gould. Skeffington. London. 1877.

New Anglican Edition of Hymns Old and New by Kevin Mayhew. 1996

New Survey of England. Devon by W.G. Hoskins. Collins, London 1959.

Newsletters of The Baring Gould Appreciation Society.

Noemi a story of rock-dwellers by S. Baring-Gould. Methuen & Co. London 1895.

Notes & Impressions of Lew Trenchard Manor by H.R. Smallcombe, Plymouth 1961.

Now The Day Is Over The Life and Times of Sabine Baring-Gould by Harold Kirk-Smith. Richard Kay. Lincolnshire. 1997.

Old English Home and its Dependencies by S Baring-Gould. Methuen & Co. London 1898.

One Hundred Sermon Sketches for Extempore Preachers. J. Master London 1871.

Onward Christian Soldier. A life of Baring-Gould by W.E. Purcell. Longmans Green & Co. London 1957.

Origin and Development of Religious Belief by S. Baring-Gould Vols 1&2 by Rivingtons, London 1869/70.

Ossett Observer 13 June 1903.

Our Friend the Charlatan by G Gissing. Chapman & Hall. 1901.

Parish Church of St Peter, Lew Trenchard, by SBG & Bickford Dickinson 3rd impression. Sunfire Press. Tavistock 1972

Path of the Just. Tales of Holy Men and Children By S. Baring-Gould. J. Masters.1854.

Pennycomequicks. Spencer Blackett & Hallam 1889.

Persons of Consequence. Queen Victoria and Her Circle by Louis Auchincloss. Weidenfeld & Nicolson. London 1979.

Preacher's Pocket: a packet of sermons. Skeffington & Son London 1880.

Private Papers of Henry Ryecroft by George Gissing. Constable. London 1921.

Pulpits by S. Baring-Gould. Sunday Magazine, Vol.24.

R.L. Arundale papers. West Yorkshire Archive Service

Recollections of my Grandfather, Sabine Baring-Gould, my Grandmother and my early childhood by Joyce Rawstorn 1992. By kind permission of Sue Murray.

Religion and Society in Industrial England by Alan D. Gilbert. Longman. London.

Royal Institute of Cornwall Journal X1 by S. Baring-Gould.

Sabine Baring-Gould. Squarson, Writer & Folklorist by Bickford H. C. Dickinson. David & Charles. Newton Abbot 1970.

Sermons to Children by S. Baring-Gould. Skeffington. London 1879.

Silver Store. Poems collected from Medieval Christian & Jewish Mines by S. Baring-Gould. Longmans, London. 1868.

Small World of Fred Hoyle. Michael Joseph. 1986.

Songs of the West by S. Baring-Gould, H. Fleetwood Sheppard & F.W. Bussell, under the Musical Editorship of Cecil J. Sharp. 6th Ed. in 1 Vol. Methuen & Co. London 1922. Notes on Songs p.9.

Strange Survivals & Superstitions by S. Baring-Gould. Methuen London 1892.

Sunday Magazine 1895.

Sunday Magazine Vol. 24 pp.597-606 September 1895.

Sunday Round. Plain village sermons for the Sundays of the Christian year (4vols). Skeffington & Son London 1898/9.

The Chorister. A Tale of King's College Chapel in the Civil War Anonymous [S. Baring-Gould]. J.P.Gray 1856.

The Church in Germany by S. Baring-Gould. Wells Gardner, Darton & Co. London 1891.

Them Days by Joy Lakeman from the memories of Joan Bellan. Tabb House, Padstow 1987.

The Sign, courtesy of Chansistor Publications Ltd.

Through All the Changing Scenes of Life by S. Baring-Gould. SPCK. 1892.

Through Flood and Flame. Anonymous.[S. Baring-Gould]. Richard Bentley. London 1868.

Times Newspaper 11th January 1992.

Tragedy of the Caesars' by S. Baring-Gould. Methuen. London1892.

Trollope by Victoria Glendinning. Pimlico 1993.

Troubadour Land (Provence & Languedoc) by S. Baring-Gould. W.H.Allen & Co. London 1891.

Unattributed press cutting dated 29 January 192?

Venn Cambridge.

Vicar of Morwenstowe, Being a life of Robert Stephen Hawker, M.A. by S. Baring-Gould. Henry S. King. London 1876.

Village Preaching for A Year Vol 11. Skeffington.1875.

Wakefield Express.

Yorkshire Archaeological Society Journal 1913.

Yorkshire Notes & Queries with Folklore Journal Vol.11. 1890.

Yorkshire Oddities, Incidents and Strange Events by S. Baring-Gould. Hodges 1874 & 1987 in abridged form by Smith Settle.

Yorkshire Post 27 March 1997 - Baker's Yorkshire.

Young Man Magazine 1895.

Index

Index

Index